ABOUT TH

C000259189

Jason Francis is the creator of t
in Cornwall, Jason left home at ~~10 to attend drama school in~~
Guildford. In 2001, frustrated at not getting acting roles, he
wrote a play about 1960s playwright Joe Orton and cast himself
in the main role. It ran in London for four weeks and lost him
thousands, and *The Times* described his acting as 'ordinary'.

In 1997, he moved from acting into producing, and formed
Premier Stage Productions Ltd, which grew into one of the world's
largest children's theatre touring companies, staging international
tours of *Thomas the Tank Engine*, *Bob the Builder* and *Sesame
Street*, to name but a few. In 2013, he met entrepreneur Jonathan
Kendrick and joined his ROK group of companies, becoming
CEO and partner with him at Events That ROK.

Jason owns a Sports and Social Club in Newbury, called
The Crucible, and is also manager of eleven times ladies world
Snooker Champion, Reanne Evans. Jason lives in Ascot – and
occasionally plays snooker himself!

snookerlegends.co.uk
YouTube: @snookerlegends

SN⬤OKER LEGENDS

ON THE ROAD AND OFF THE TABLE
WITH SNOOKER'S GREATEST

JASON FRANCIS

JOHN BLAKE

Published by John Blake Publishing
2.25, The Plaza,
535 Kings Road,
Chelsea Harbour,
London, SW10 0SZ

www.johnblakebooks.co.uk

facebook.com/johnblakebooks
twitter.com/jblakebooks

Paperback – 978-1-78606-984-9
Ebook – 978-1-78946-030-8

A CIP catalogue of this book is available from the British Library.

Typeset by EnvyDesign Ltd
Printed and bound in Great Britain by Clays Ltd, Elcograf S.p.A.

1 3 5 7 9 10 8 6 4 2

John Blake Publishing is an imprint of Bonnier Publishing
www.bonnierpublishing.co.uk

For my grandpa, Clifford Hocking, who first put a snooker cue in my hand and always found two shillings for the light.

For Jimmy, Ronnie, Cliff and all the snooker legends who stuck by me on this crazy journey.

For Mum, Dad and Ross, it turned out OK.

And for Michelle – you make me laugh every single day.

CONTENTS

FOREWORD

During 2016 I spent more time with Jason than with my girlfriend. We smashed the exhibitions that year as well as playing some tournaments. Since he started with me we've had some great times; yeah, he was there when I won a few masters, UK's and a World's, but I'm talking about the laughs on the road, the late-night driving back from a show after midnight raiding a service station for every Krispy Kreme donut they have and making me listen to his crap music.

I call him the boomerang as no matter what is thrown at him he keeps coming back. He's been good for me and I think I've been good for him. When I got ill after playing Gilbert in the World Champs, he helped get me out of Sheffield, drove me down to London and stayed with me until I was safe with my family. During that week, while I concentrated on getting better, he worked behind the scenes in secret, getting my cue fixed and avoiding the press who all wanted to know where I was.

I know he wanted to concentrate on building a seniors tour so it was great that our last proper event together in York was a winning one. He's worked hard to get Snooker Legends where it is, never giving up when things got tough.

I know he'll do anything for me and I also know he'll have me up and down the motorway knocking out exhibitions every chance he gets. We have a saying that none of it really matters, as long as you can get your poached eggs in the morning, every day can be a good day.

Good friend, good mate and he has my back, enough said.

Ronnie O'Sullivan,
July 2018

MARCH 2010 –
MATCHROOM SPORT HQ

*'I don't think you're going to make enough money for me to
fuck you over, so I'll let you do it.'*
BARRY HEARN, NEW CHAIRMAN OF WORLD SNOOKER LTD

CHAPTER 1

TWO SHILLINGS FOR THE METER

I'm just a very average snooker player with a background in theatre who decided to create an event I would buy tickets to myself.

Back in the 1970s a lot of families were poor. It didn't make them unhappy but it meant they had to make choices and budget for essentials in a way people don't now. For me, we could only watch the television if we had two shillings to put in the meter on the back; for my mum and dad it was a way of ensuring that when the rental had to be paid on the TV, the money was there. It did, however, mean that sometimes my snooker coverage went off-air, my screen replaced with darkness rather than an episode of *Hairy Bikers* or *Coast* like it is today. The frustration was the same though.

I'd watch snooker with my grandfather, a navy veteran of the Russian convoys. Despite the limitations of money I saw enough to learn the nicknames and study the styles of the top boys. Hurricane, Whirlwind, Grinder – I was mesmerised by their flamboyance, their champagne lifestyles and their fame.

I badgered my grampa to take me to the snooker hall and eventually came to own my own cue: EJ Riley, Joe Davis one-piece, in ash, it was a beauty.

Childhood memories are scarce but my first visit to play a game of snooker on a full-size table with Grandpa Hocking is vivid. After my mate's six foot by three it felt like a football field. I wasn't even sure I could hit the ball that far, but I was hooked. From 13 to 16, that place, in the Men's Institute, was a second home to me and my friends. Daily routine: in from school, quick change, out the door, 'Bye Mum', off to the snooker room. I'd only return when darkness descended or we could no longer blag money for the light from one of the older boys.

Cherished moments of our time together in that snooker room left a lasting impression on me; no doubt the tobacco cloud probably did too. Happy times, lifelong friendships, all based around a twelve by six foot piece of furniture.

By the time I left home at 18, I'd already secured the County Under 21 Snooker title, but I wasn't leaving home to play snooker: I wanted to be an actor.

I wanted a better life than my parents had; it hurt me seeing them struggle to try and not let me or my brother go without. I made a promise that it wouldn't just be at Christmas time I got to drink something called 'pop'.

In 1998 both my parents died. I was just 28 and felt alone, vulnerable. I channelled my grief and anger into determination and drive, not always getting it right, in fact getting it wrong on many occasions, but I learned and listened and refused to give up.

In 2001, frustrated at not getting any acting roles, I wrote a play about 1960s playwright Joe Orton and cast myself in the main role. It ran in London for four weeks and lost me thousands, and *The Times* described my acting as 'ordinary'.

Years of debt, too many early mornings delivering newspapers and too many late nights serving pizzas, cold walks home because I couldn't afford a bus, and growing my hair long because I couldn't afford to have it cut.

There was no silver spoon, no helping hand, but there was determination to get up every time I was knocked down.

I never thought that an idea to stage a snooker exhibition with my hero Alex Higgins in 2010 would, within three years, grow into an event that was watched by more than 12 million on Eurosport.

I never thought I'd be able to one day call Ronnie O'Sullivan and Jimmy White my good friends.

I never knew where this crazy idea would take me.

I just dared to dream... and never gave up.

CHAPTER 2

CRISIS PART 1: WORLD CHAMPIONSHIP, R1

18th April 2016

RONNIE O'SULLIVAN 10 V DAVE GILBERT 7

I managed to snatch the back of the cue just after it had been rammed into the breeze-block wall of dressing-room three for a second time; splintered and split, it had definitely played its last frame. By now the little plastic disc with 'John Parris Ultimate Cue' etched into it was rolling around the dressing-room floor, everything was going at 100mph and yet there was silence.

Ronnie was broken, as low as I'd ever seen him, the crazy thing being he had just won. He went for a wee, door open as usual, and using his left hand to steady the flow he subsequently smashed his right fist into the toilet wall.

The silence broke. 'I can't do this any more, Jase, it's too much.' I held him in my arms, a grown man sobbing like a child. He had cracked and what's worse, we were trapped together in an eight by six dressing room with the world's media huddled in the corridor just outside.

A knock at the door. I opened it a feather to see Damien Hirst and Antony Genn at the front of a hoard, cameras already clicking past me hoping to grab a snapshot of the carnage within.

Despite the seriousness of the moment it reminded me of how the press run alongside prison vans holding up their lenses at a blacked-out window – we felt like prisoners.

Damien was always with us at the major events, his friendship with Ronnie well documented; Antony goes way back with Damien and is best known from the pop groups The Hours, Pulp and Elastica... or perhaps for getting naked on stage at Glastonbury in 2005, a stunt which he later blamed on an 'astronomical amount of drugs'!

I let Damien in but gave Antony a look which meant stand down for a minute. We now know people heard the symphony of 'cue on wall' from outside. Of course the media turned it into a headline about smashing up the whole dressing room like he had morphed into Keith Moon or Liam Gallagher. The only thing broken was a snooker cue and a set of knuckles, both owned by the world's most famous snooker player who was at this moment sobbing uncontrollably into the world's most famous artist's arms in a room with a failed actor from Cornwall. I've been in some weird situations over the years but this was right up there.

Under the terms of their World Snooker players' contract, all match winners have to attend a press conference, and sometimes they appear live on TV right after the match, the so-called 'flash' interview. I know this is fairly consistent across all live sports but I'm never sure if it is always necessary, especially when a player who has given everything on the field, or in this case table, is emotionally and physically spent. In our sport the players tread a very fine line between what is considered OK to talk about and what the contract dictates they can't. Now if the person interviewing you is from World Snooker, then of course they are not going to knowingly lead a player into an area where they could criticise the sport, the authorities or tournament conditions... But if it's the host broadcaster, or independent journalists looking for their story, the temptation sometimes is too much to ignore, especially when they know that Ronnie is always honest, always emotional and likely to give them a payday or a sound bite their editor will snap up.

I knew he couldn't face the press; he was struggling to face us. He was in complete meltdown and I am not being in any way dramatic. I also knew the press were waiting, and by that I don't just mean in the corridor outside, or assembled in the media room, but globally the host broadcasters and all fans wanted, no – actually expected, to hear him speak about the match – this was the World Snooker Championship.

I also was very aware of what would happen if we didn't do any press. Column inches have to be filled and on many occasions I've discussed with Ronnie that we are better to give them our version, his actual words, rather than allow them to create their own sensationalism. By not talking we were going to create a bigger story than doing so… but this was a time to put my player first and let them do their worst.

I poked my head around the door and announced to the press officer that we weren't doing any press.

The first response from Ivan, the World Snooker media officer, was 'You know it's a fine', which disappointed me a bit. A simple 'Is he OK?', or even 'What's wrong?' would have been more appropriate, but then again I understood he had a job to do and he was probably under pressure and knew he'd be the one having to relay the news that Ronnie O'Sullivan was refusing to attend his press conference. The message should really have been 'unable to attend' not 'refusing to'.

The truth was that Ronnie O'Sullivan was barely coherent and couldn't stand. He needed me to be crystal clear in my thinking; he needed proper medical care. I don't feel I am betraying any trust now recounting these events, as Ronnie has himself spoken about them over the previous 12 months, most recently to Victoria Derbyshire on BBC *Breakfast*. Everything I write about in this book has either already been reported, or is less damaging but more interesting to the readers. Quite often most of what is reported is inaccurate; therefore I'm happy to be able to put the record straight.

I was aware that we'd been in the dressing room for at least 15 minutes, three prisoners needing to plan an escape; all that was missing was Steve McQueen, James Garner and someone to dig 'Tom, Dick and Harry'.

Everything was still a bit of a blur. I understood I now had to take over the situation and keep my client safe. What I did notice was that the hordes of fans at the stage door were incredibly respectful, very unlike the hungry journalists that had laid siege to the dressing room. It was 'Are you OK, Ronnie?', 'Go on the rocket', 'Take care, Ronnie', with not really anyone invading his personal space to ask for signatures or photos. I sensed, like me, they knew it was serious...

For me the tournament was over, but the bigger question was whether his snooker career was too?

CHAPTER 3

INTO THE EYE OF A HURRICANE

Citywest Hotel, Dublin: November 2009

It was the early flight out of Stansted, the 'red eye' Ryanair flight into Dublin, so called because most of the passengers have been up half of the night to make sure they don't miss it. As usual, with this particular budget airline, the queues were horrendous; people were being made to pack and unpack their suitcases and because they were carrying one business card too many they were being charged an extra £40 in excess baggage. Tempers were rising, it was a crappy, cold November's morning barely breaking freezing, but I didn't care. Amid the turmoil and revolutionary atmosphere I was happy. Why? Because I was off to meet my hero and I'd just found out the snooker show I was putting him in was already sold out!

Alex 'Hurricane' Higgins was the reason I started playing snooker. The swagger, the grace, the sheer arrogance of this man who seemed to have a blatant disregard for authority of any kind, captivated a nation. This included one chubby 12-year-old boy in Cornwall, who watched as Alex cried and cradled his young daughter Lauren after winning the 1982 World Snooker Championship.

Alex was different; he was box office. A genius? Well, compared to a man who performs life-saving surgery, no, but by God he could play snooker, and play it in a way the world had never seen.

Alex Higgins, and his possible participation, was the main reason I created the Snooker Legends Tour. Alex Higgins, and the fact I sacked him after just one show, is the reason Snooker Legends is now one of the world's largest independent snooker promotions.

With him it was created; without him it was able to continue...

A bout of earache meant I missed the chance to see him play at a local leisure centre when I was just 11; my mate Gary's dad got me his autograph though. Little did Alex know that this particular signature, one of hundreds he would have given on the night, would be for a child who would one day employ him and take him back to the Crucible Theatre to play his last ever snooker exhibition. Ironic really.

Alex was my favourite player but Jimmy White was close behind. Jimmy was young, just coming on the scene. He looked like a rock star and I wanted his perm. I wasn't so keen on Cliff Thorburn: he was so slow and based his game on stopping Alex and Jimmy expressing themselves. Kirk Stevens was someone else I supported, whereas Steve Davis was easily the best at that time but berated on programmes like *Spitting Image* for being 'not interesting'. I can't remember what I thought of him at that time, if truth be told.

I'd been warned by Jimmy about meeting Alex, and the legendary tricks and stunts he could pull. The route to meeting Alex had to come through Jimmy, and the route to Jimmy had to go through his manager at the time, Double K, Kevin Kelly.

The first meeting with Kevin was at Epsom Golf Club where I intended to use the booking of Jimmy for my local league's presentation night as a vehicle to introduce him to the idea of a Legends Tour. My idea was to replicate what they had done in Golf and Tennis for their retired legendary performers. I thought there was a gap in the market, I just needed a catalyst to get it going.

There is no doubt this man came into Jimmy's life at a time when 'The Whirlwind' needed him. There is also no doubt that the next five to six years, and the way they lived their lives, played a part in Jimmy's decline in the rankings.

They travelled the country in an over-aged Mercedes, making a few quid here and there, playing exhibitions in anything from the finest hotels and casinos to the grubbiest of clubs. The lovely thing about Jimmy, and you will see numerous references to this later, is that he doesn't regret a moment of it – they had a lot of fun, made a lot of money, and who needs a spare wheel or a change of clothes in the boot when that space can be taken up by a few old black-and-white photos of Jimmy and Alex that Kevin can flog for a tenner?

Jimmy had to earn money; his outgoings and commitments were huge. Five children, an ex-wife, a young girlfriend on his arm and flash cars cost money, and it wasn't coming in from tournament winnings. Jimmy and Kevin were the masters – it really was Del Boy and Rodney. The problem was the more they earned, the more they spent. I'm not judging them, and not one bit of this is Kevin's fault, but it almost cost Jimmy his job as a professional snooker player. The saviour came in 2009, in the form of the Australian outback and a TV show called *I'm a Celebrity... Get Me Out of Here*, hosted by a Geordie duo by the name of Ant and Dec. It seems as if the offer to go to Australia for a TV show, and the creation of the Legends Tour, came along at just the right time for The Whirlwind.

The first time I promised to deliver a show at the Crucible they both collectively ridiculed me – Jimmy and Kevin that is, not Ant and Dec. As Jimmy says in his own book, they thought it was a scam. By the time I produced the proof of the Crucible contract, they had both agreed to become joint promoters, taking part of the business, and any profit, in return for delivering Alex.

I thought that making Jimmy a partner, and including Kevin in a share of profits, would tie them in long term, and, more importantly, give me a buffer for the antics of Alex.

Alex listened to no one, but if anyone could get through to him on some level, it was going to be Jimmy. Jimmy travelled the country doing exhibitions with Alex. The general consensus was that Jimmy was the only person who would work with Alex – but don't be fooled. Jimmy knew having Alex on the bill guaranteed ticket sales, and large ticket sales guaranteed large merchandise sales! Jimmy has been called many things over his 35-year career; stupid is not one of them.

Kevin had met a new lady and was moving to Cork to run an organic vegetable farm. How on earth he thought he could co-promote a Legends Tour was beyond me, especially as he seemed to have a real problem answering a phone. Then again, he was hardly Alan Titchmarsh either. Nevertheless, he was tasked with getting Alex to sign the contract.

Alex's Legend contract detailed £18,000 for 18 appearances; it was more money than he had earned playing snooker for a long time and it would be drip fed as we went along, to the delight of me but not Paddy Power, I suspect.

Jimmy going into *I'm a Celebrity... Get Me Out of Here* on ITV that winter meant that he would miss the UK Championship, a huge event in the snooker calendar. That decision told me two things:

1. Jimmy thought he could no longer win the UK Championship.
2. The money offered to live in squalor with Katie Price and cockroaches for a few weeks was too good to turn down.

For me it was great timing. Say what you like about these reality shows but they give the people involved a huge profile boost, and they pay well. Of course, in return, you get to eat kangaroo cock and not shower for three weeks!

During my time with Ronnie he's been offered all the reality shows – the Jungle, *Strictly* and most recently *Dancing On Ice*. We've also been offered *Celebrity Big Brother* and I think if he ever does go down that road, it's that particular one that will appeal most.

I think in the end Jimmy surprised even himself, finishing third, and making some good friendships with Hollywood film star George Hamilton and chef Gino D'Acampo.

Jimmy's girlfriend at the time, Kelly, had travelled with him to Australia and spent three weeks in the Versace five-star hotel while he shat daily in an oil drum – not a bad way to impress your bird either, I suppose!

About this time, our first shows went on sale and the news broke of a Snooker Legends Tour being created. The Crucible show sold out in about is due at the end of 2018 is due at the end of 2018 hours. Alex going back was enough to guarantee that, but with the added incentive of him playing Thorburn there again, and Jimmy there as well, it was big news.

A day before I travelled to Dublin to meet Alex for the first time, I delivered the news of the sell-out to all the players. Michaela Tabb, the high profile lady referee I had booked, was delighted, Jimmy ws stunned and Alex said, 'Babes you should have charged double – they would have paid it for me.' He was probably right!

I arrived at Citywest about 10am, Alex was due at 11. In the days between the story breaking and this trip, I'd been contacted by Jim White (no relation) from the *Telegraph* wanting to do an exclusive interview with Alex.

Within their contracts all the players have an obligation to help promote and advertise the shows at no cost to me. No chance with Alex. He wanted 1,000 euros, the *Telegraph* offered 300, we settled on 500 – in cash of course... and saved on unnecessary paperwork!

The camera crews set up; the public at the hotel were asking what was going on. News that a Hurricane was due to hit the hotel had already created quite a buzz. Jimmy told me he'd be late, I'd warned everyone. I was on edge, but Jim White was relaxed, explaining he'd interviewed George Best and Oliver Reed so he was able to handle Alex.

I was ready, I had 300 euros in cash ready to cover any eventuality – all I needed was for this day to go smoothly, in some ways for me to weather the Hurricane.

At 11am a cab pulled up outside the hotel... It was Alex 'Sandy' Higgins, bang on time.

I was prepared for the physical state he would be in, I was prepared to be hit with the cab bill (and of course I was), I was prepared to stick to my guns and not pay any more money than was in the contract we had signed... What I was not prepared for, when I held my hand out to shake his, was the full kiss on the lips I got. 'Hello, babes... you owe me 60 euros for the cab.' He put me on the back foot straight away. I was gone. Snooker's royalty had arrived in Dublin, and he was demanding that every protocol be followed.

I had brought Steve Smart who worked in my office with me; he was visibly shocked at this skeleton of a man in front of me. Alex was very thin, but his mind was sharp and he was holding court.

We'd arranged to go down to Palmerston House, the private residence of Citywest owner Jimmy Mansfield and a place I would later use as a base for the players during our events in Goffs in Kildare. We'd do a photo shoot there, as it had a snooker table, and then return to the hotel to record the interview for the *Telegraph*.

Everyone was getting photographs with Alex. I desperately wanted one, too, but had to try to remain cool: he already had me at a disadvantage. In 2009 the 'selfie' was still not yet the chosen choice of quick portrait.

Steve, Alex and I sat at a table. Alex had brought me a gift, a gift! It was a black-and-white photo of him from 1974 that wasn't in circulation. He said I could get it copied and we could sell them at the shows as no one would have it. I was thrilled, then of course he said, 'And I only want five euros a piece for them.'

Alex wanted to talk about the tour. I asked Steve to fetch out the current tour dates and details. 'No need,' said Alex, as he already had the full dates and venues written on three betting slips, one for May, June and July. Next to the Crucible date were the words SOLD OUT – I feared the worst.

I'd already been fleeced for a cab fare, and a first-class train ticket from Belfast soon followed. He wanted to know if the *Telegraph* had brought cash for the interview, but then to my amazement started suggesting we did a show in Ulster Hall in Belfast and a venue in Blackburn he had played at.

After Alex had had a pint of Guinness, with a quick rum chaser, we travelled down to Palmerston House. Alex reminded me that he needed to put on our branded shirt with the Snooker Legends logo – he wanted a private room to change in and once the door had closed it was just the two of us.

For five minutes the façade dropped. It wasn't easy to have any conversation with Alex as the throat cancer had ravaged his vocal cords; all he could manage was a quiet rasp. It was difficult to understand and obviously any speech was painful for him. I later learned it was the scarring from the chemotherapy.

I gingerly helped him out of his full-length coat and long-sleeved shirt and we put the Snooker Legends polo shirt on. I was shocked at the state of him: not so much the malnutrition, as you could see that through his clothes, but that his upper body was covered in scars and what I can only guess were liver spots. He saw I was shocked and broke the silence. 'Don't worry, babes, I'm still breathing.' I laughed almost in embarrassment; the man who once showed unbelievable strength of character in the face of adversity now didn't have the strength to lift his arms above his head to put on a polo shirt.

Sadly, even he agreed that the small size hung off him like a bin bag and his forearms were in a bad way, so we put his shirt back on to cover his arms and the T-shirt went on top. I'd like to say 'polo shirt on top of long-sleeved Oxford shirt' was simply a Higgins new season fashion for 2009 – but we weren't kidding anybody.

Alex shuffled into the games room and what I can only describe as a miracle took place. Almost immediately his eyes switched on, he stood up straight, and headed straight for the cue rack. 'Let's have a frame.'

The Hurricane was back at a snooker table. The security blanket was twelve foot by six, and the shuffling soon became a swagger. The lights had to be moved: we'd only been planning to take a few shots at the table but now Alex wanted a game... and I was going to be his opponent!

The *Telegraph* crew were protesting to Jim White about the time it would take and how this wasn't in the schedule. White wasn't stupid. He told them to put the normal photo cameras away and get the film cameras out – Alex Higgins playing snooker was something you didn't really see any more.

I was a bit stunned to be honest. The table was old, the cloth threadbare and the balls resembled a box of oranges, but was I going to turn down this chance to play him? No way.

There were four cues in the rack. Two didn't have tips; one had a tip that looked like a blueberry muffin; one tip looked pretty decent. Alex, of course, took the only decent cue in the rack; after all, this was going to be all about him. To tell the truth, I'd have played him with a broom handle.

I had the break-off; the camera crew were rearranging their equipment. Alex was busy banging the shaft of the cue he had chosen on his palm, apparently checking its stiffness.

Whereas most players use maybe one or two cues throughout the whole of their careers, I believe Alex had dozens. Was he always looking for perfection? Maybe, but I'm sure many had to be replaced after being broken across someone's shoulders or lost as collateral in a card game in one or more Belfast watering holes.

I was shitting myself. I was a fair player in my youth but in this situation, with this table, and a tip like a soggy marshmallow, I feared the worst. I broke off, touch of right-hand side, hit the fourth red and came back inside the blue, nestled perfectly frozen against the top cushion. I looked around. I'd played perhaps the perfect break-off, but was anyone looking? Not a chance. People were messing about with camera leads and lights, and Alex was still using the natural light of the window to inspect the ferrule on his cue. I'm sure I could have placed the ball there by hand and no one would have noticed.

I handed the only piece of chalk to Alex. I wouldn't be seeing it again. He had no shot; the only red he could see was tight on the cushion just past the middle pocket. He could either clip thin off the edge of it and play what we call a 'dump shot', or come off a cushion and drop into the pack.

What he couldn't do was roll the red four feet up the cushion and drop it dead weight into the corner bag. The place went mad – of course now every fucker was watching. Alex just grinned. 'Never lose it, babes,' he rasped.

We played for 15 minutes and Alex was happy to pause on shots for them to get a good camera angle. He probably made the odd 20, nothing spectacular.

I made a couple of colours but had to pick them myself – our friendship wasn't blossoming that much! It was obvious he was lacking any cue power but the touch and feel were still there, even on this table. The lighting was very poor, and the cameramen were having to supplement it to get any sort of image. It didn't bother Alex – 'I grew up playing in the dark,' he remarked.

At the end of the game we wanted to do some photos at the

front of the house. I put my cue in the rack, Alex held on to his. 'I like this cue, it has potential, I'm having it,' he announced.

The housekeeper at Palmerston House looked a bit flustered. 'I'm sorry, Mr Higgins, but that's Mr Mansfield's personal cue, so I can't let it go.'

The reply was genius: 'Get Mr Mansfield on the phone, and tell him Mr Higgins wants his cue, and I'm not taking no for an answer.'

She was unmoved, far braver than I would be. 'Sorry, Mr Higgins, but I can't do that as Mr Mansfield is on holiday, but if you'd like to call him next week…'

She went on talking, but by that time Alex had thrown the cue on the table and headed up the stairs outside for the photo shoot. She'd verbally sparred with Alex and won; I almost wanted to take her on tour. I wish I had done.

The cue's rightful owner, Jimmy Mansfield, was a pretty formidable character. According to a 2003 report, when he sold 100,000 tonnes of machinery, which had been left over from the Falklands War, *The Irish Times* estimated the profit at £19m in the US and a further £7m in the UK. He realised that land was going up in value in Ireland in the early 1990s, and he successfully secured several thousand acres near Saggart, County Dublin. He successfully turned this land into the Citywest Hotel and built the private residence we were currently using for the shoot. He carried on dealing in his machinery trade, which once again added to his wealth, amounting to a reputed €200m as of 21 February, 2010. But he wasn't Alex Higgins, was he?

The photo shoot went relatively smoothly, mostly because the bloke was petrified and Higgins ran the show, telling him where to stand and how to take the photo.

Before we left, Alex asked to use the bathroom, and while we got into our cars, and said our thanks, he popped back inside. After about five minutes I sent the *Telegraph* car on ahead back to Citywest to set up for the main interview. What on earth was Alex doing?

Our host went back through the front door to see if he was OK. Once she was out of sight, Alex appeared from round the side of the building and got in the back of the car with me. It felt like the sort of prison break that Michael Scofield and Lincoln Burrows would have been proud of.

It was only when we got out of the gate that he opened his coat to reveal Jimmy Mansfield's cue – Alex was having it after all, but to add insult to injury he only wanted the top half, so was going to cut it in half and dispose of the butt! I'm not sure Jimmy Mansfield ever found out – sadly he passed away in January 2014 – and he may not have cared. His housekeeper was last seen searching his stately home for a missing Hurricane and her boss' snooker cue!

Once back at Citywest, the euros were handed over and Jim White got his interview. As far as I know it was the last interview Alex ever did, and as shocking as his physical appearance was, you can see the fire still burned when he talked about snooker.

He claimed he could still have been in the top 32, which was folly. The aura and arrogance were still there, but physically I doubted he could have managed more than two or three frames. I was worried. In my opinion there was no way he could currently sustain an 18-date national tour with the Legends.

Had I made a terrible mistake?

CHAPTER 4

MEETING BARRY

I can't remember exactly when I first had the idea for a Legends Tour. Many people have asked me, and it would be great to create some symbolic 'light bulb' moment. However, the truth, as far as I can remember, was I'd been bored shitless watching Peter Ebdon and Graeme Dott on TV take an hour over each frame – and the children's theatre company I owned was beginning to feel the bite of the recession. I was looking at ways to use our position and contacts with the theatres to try out another type of show.

Snooker Legends was one idea I had and recreating the Sunday-night darts game show *Bullseye* was another. (I actually produced the *Bullseye* theatre tour as well, in 2010: it sank faster than the imaginary speedboat they offered on it for the 101 or more in six darts!)

I didn't pick snooker out of the air as a subject for a new show. As I mentioned earlier, the game had been in my blood from a young age. I didn't actually pick up a cue until I was 14, but I won the Cornwall Under-21 championship just three years later.

I lived in a small rural village in Cornwall called Mount Hawke, a village without a pub but with a Men's and Women's Institute. It always amazed me that I could visit the Women's Institute at any age but wasn't allowed in the Men's until I was fourteen. The Women's Institute offered coffee mornings, whist drives and talks on gardening. The Men's Institute had a full-size snooker table!

At the time Jimmy went into the Jungle with Ant and Dec (autumn 2009), the world of snooker was changing. In just a matter of weeks Rodney Walker, his huge salary and six tournaments a year was gone, and the self-proclaimed messiah, who had spent most of the last ten years at loggerheads with the sport, was back. Enter Barry Hearn.

The sport was in a mess and although Barry said he had unfinished business, that was bollocks. Barry Hearn saw an opportunity to make a lot of money and acquire the sport that for so many years he had been fighting. People with far longer memories than me immediately voiced their concerns, but the truth was he was the only viable option, although I believe he only got in by a couple of players' votes?

The World Professional Billiards and Snooker Accounts (WPBSA) showed a cash balance of around £600,000 in 2009, nowhere near enough for the governing body to operate globally. Jason Ferguson managed to get 26 per cent for the WPBSA, but it's reported the rest was snapped up by Barry for about a quid. The commercial rights to the game were sold for less than it takes to pay for the light to play a frame in many clubs today.

You can't blame Barry: they went begging to him and he named his terms. I'm surprised they even got a pound out of him for it. It was great business for his company Matchroom Sport. Shrewd.

Jump forward eight years to 2017 and it's reported a recent approach by an investment firm to buy Matchroom Sport got quoted a £500m asking price. Now I accept that World Snooker Ltd may only be a part of the Matchroom portfolio, but that's still great business. You will of course be told there is more money in the sport than ever before; you'll be told that snooker is now being watched globally by more people than ever before. Both are true, but are you seriously telling me that snooker is now a bigger sport than it was in the 1980s? It may be getting there financially but it's not there yet, and a certain game played with a modern version of an inflated pig's bladder now completely dominates sport globally.

The top ten players in that 1980s golden era of snooker were all superstars earning the equivalent of a million pounds a year. At its height Barry managed most of them; the problem he has now is the game's only global superstar is Ronnie O'Sullivan – and he's a loose cannon. Sure he has Ding Junhui, the most popular sportsman in China, but that relationship is only on slightly thicker ice than his one with Ronnie. He desperately needs Judd Trump or a young Chinese kid to win the World Championship to take the emphasis on the commercial value of the sport away from those two mavericks.

To be fair, what Barry immediately did was give the game credibility again. He had already built the PDC Darts Tour in to a money-making machine, and he wasted no time in telling the players that their holiday was over. If they wanted to be full-time professional sportsmen, then they better get used to playing more than eight weeks a year. The 2010 calendar was completely restructured, with the introduction of 12 Player Tour Championship events, or PTCs as they were commonly known.

I immediately had a problem, as I had 18 Legends dates booked and on sale, and now Jimmy White would be required to play in these new tournaments at the same time.

The PTCs were initially widely welcomed: they were shorter tournaments played over only three days and offered a 10K winner's prize. It gave countries that couldn't fund or stage a full-ranking tournament a chance to get the top players into their territories. With a field of 128 it was dog eat dog, but what people didn't see was that by allowing the amateurs to enter these tournaments, with the chance of maybe getting that plum tie against a top pro, Barry rang the death knell for the English amateur game, and to a lesser extent the International Billiards Snooker Federation (IBSF) who at that time still represented the only route snooker had to the Holy Grail – Olympic status.

Top amateurs trying to break through into the tour no longer invested in grass-roots amateur snooker and the cheques were made out to Barry instead, with a route to tour status now only possible from their own ranking list. Even now in 2017 I don't think people realise what happened.

Three-day events, best of seven matches throughout, random draws... and a hell of a lot more hours of content for Bazza to sell to TV. Double shrewd!

We've now almost waved goodbye to the PTC events – in Barry's words, they've served their purpose – but details have emerged of a new amateur series of events in which you will only be able to play if you've already parted with £1000 for Q school. In 2018, about 300 players entered Q school, a cool 300k in entry fees in return for 12 tour cards. Worth doing, eh? Especially as he will probably sell the extra content to TV as well. Well I guess he had to get back the money he lost by giving the 128 professional tour players free tournament entries somehow, didn't he?

Barry is very lucky that he has a multiple world champion in Mark Selby, who is a perfect ambassador for the sport. Shaun Murphy is the same – these two will answer the call to represent the sport at short notice whenever Barry calls them, sometimes they may even get their flight paid for too.

Barry can bring more money into the sport than before; he can deliver new opportunities and new territories. However, what he can't do is make the game's most marketable commodity, Ronnie, travel to play in them.

There is more money, but there are also more mouths to feed with 128 professionals. There is only one person at the top of the rankings in snooker earnings, and he doesn't even play the game. Accounts will show Barry earned more from snooker last year than Mark Selby and Ronnie O'Sullivan combined, but then again he'd say at nearly 70 years old he's worth it. You can't help but admire him.

Because of the tournament clashes I had to go and meet with Barry. I think for him it was about sizing up the opposition. He had taken control of World Snooker Ltd, he had seized the German and World Series events, and he had created the PTC tour. The Legends Tour was probably the only thing in snooker he hadn't yet taken control of – but then again we hadn't yet even staged a show.

I went with Nick George, who at the time was my fellow director at my theatre company. We were shown into Matchroom Sport's offices in Brentwood, which I believe was once Barry's home, we took our seats outside his office. Barry's office door was open. Maybe that's standard, maybe it was staged, but we both listened to someone getting the bollocking of their lives.

Nick and I looked at each other. It was quite intimidating and there was only one voice being heard, and it was up to full volume.

Out of the office came shuffling the man I now know to have been Pat Mooney, a newly appointed World Snooker Director, and manager of top player John Higgins. He looked embarrassed as he made eye contact with us, knowing that we had heard every word. We both walked into Barry's office ready for Round Two – *ding ding!*

A warm handshake followed and it was hard to believe the calm, softly spoken, jovial Eastender was the same monster who had destroyed the previous visitor to the office. I arrived with gifts – photos from the early 1980s supplied by our Legends photographer who had taken them at the Crucible at the time – and in return we got coffee. It was all very pleasant.

'So tell me about it, boys,' he asked, and like a naïve schoolboy

I ended up revealing every detail of our tour, from ticket prices to touring costs and theatre deals. The only thing I didn't divulge was the player's wages, although, trust me, he was angling for it.

He asked a lot about Alex Higgins. At the time I thought he was showing compassion for Alex's well-publicised ill-health; I now think he was telling me that without Higgins to sell the tickets I'd be in trouble, and that by having Higgins I was guaranteed a different sort of trouble anyway!

At the end of the meeting came the quote that forms the opening of this book, and it's one I've repeated many times. He said to me: 'I like it, but I don't think you're going to make enough money for me to fuck you over, so I'll let you do it.'

I was in shock. I hadn't come to ask permission, but left there grateful for getting it, if that makes sense? I was no match for Barry that day, and I'm probably not much better at it now.

True to his word, Barry helped with the clashes, and Jimmy's qualifying matches were scheduled around the shows.

Over the past few years Barry has always made time to meet with me. At a recent meeting he acknowledged that if he hadn't come along, and snooker had continued its decline with Rodney Walker, I would have probably cleaned up. People wanted more snooker; I was going to fill that gap, but Barry came along and completely rammed it full, he took my oxygen.

When Jimmy asked me to organise his testimonial I knew that there was only one man I wanted to help and advise on it: Barry. He helped from afar, set the table prices, and used his connections to sell a few tables. I probably did 90 per cent of the work on the testimonial, but in Jimmy's book he credits Barry for it, I don't get a mention. I don't think there is any particular reason why I don't get thanked – maybe it looks better to state your testimonial was organised by the global head of the sport – it's not something I dwell on though.

In 2014 Ronnie was playing in my events instead of Barry's; it was time for a 'cup of tea' as he put it. We sat in the Waldorf and Barry sold me the idea of working together on a Legends-type show for BT Sport. He quoted getting me 100K like it was expenses money. Nothing ever came of it, and I'm not sure if it was all about letting me know he was watching me.

More recently, September 2017, I was back there again, this time trying to sort out the fact that my World Seniors Tour events had attracted UK Freeview TV and I'd already negotiated the inclusion of Jimmy White and Ken Doherty in them. That gave him a problem, but I'll save that story for a later chapter.

What is clear is that with the recent announcement of the World Snooker Seniors Tour and my partnership with the WPBSA, a collaboration suggested by him, we can now work together without any threat that what I do can in any way cannibalise or threaten his relationship with his current broadcast partners. He has said he will help and support me and I have no reason to doubt that.

In the past whenever I felt frustrated by any restriction World Snooker tried to impose on me, I asked myself a simple question: what would Barry Hearn do in my position? I have no doubt that most times he would have carried on anyway, do his events and deal with any consequences later. Some days I wish I had his fortitude. Since I first wrote this book I'm certainly a bit more Hearn and a little less Francis than I once was, but that's not necessarily a good thing!

CHAPTER 5

THE COUNTDOWN TO THE CRUCIBLE...

By February 2010 the Legends Tour was gaining momentum. I'd visited the Crucible to measure up for my theatre set, a deal had been done with BCE Riley to provide my table, and I'd met with Jimmy and Alex again at a memorabilia signing event in Coventry. Even at that event Alex had boxing legends Roberto Duran and Leon Spinks running round after him.

For a while I was brought into Alex's circle of friends, with daily phone calls asking about venues, ticket sales, constant reminders of how lucky I was to have him, and of course the obligatory demands for advances of money.

Even though it was my baby, and I had sole control, I had to create 'a phantom boss' in order to deflect and explain why I couldn't advance any monies. Not deterred by that, Alex soon found other ways for me to drip-feed him the reddies.

After the debacle of the stolen cue in Dublin, he said he needed to travel to Leeds to see a man called 'Bob' to put a new joint in it. Bob had no second name and there was no phone number forthcoming when I asked for it. Alex would need a flight into Doncaster Airport – not Leeds Bradford, which would surely have been closer? And he would need a train ticket from Doncaster to Leeds. When I suggested that perhaps it would be more convenient to fly to Leeds he told me to forget the train and he would get someone to pick him up.

I duly paid the £124 for a flight to Doncaster, only to find out later on that there was no cue man called Bob in Leeds, and the only 'cue' Alex was dealing with that day was the one to the tote at Donny Racecourse.

There is no doubt that Alex had a knowledge of horses and horse racing, but no matter how good his instincts were, the reality was he was probably a gambling addict, so actually sometimes winning was the worst thing that could happen for him. For a man who was indeed sometimes worthy of being labelled 'invincible' in his day job, it didn't take him long to believe he was unbeatable at the bookies too.

Historically gambling and snooker have gone hand in hand. For most it's about sheer boredom, and in the 1980s I believe players would regularly be seen laying a 'saver' at the bookies' stand in the venue itself. It all changed when you started being able to bet on players to lose matches; that became the issue that suddenly gave players control of their own destiny in relation to bets they may or may not have been involved in placing.

It's hard for a sport that almost solely relies on headline sponsorships from betting companies to then ask their contracted players to distance themselves from the same company that is in effect putting up the prize money. So a top player will endorse the betting sponsor proudly on his waistcoat, and lift a trophy adorned with the company coloured ribbons, but they are banned from placing bets with them? It's an issue with no easy solution.

One thing for sure is that until they totally revise the rules they will continue to catch and discipline players for retrospective gambling. It almost needs an amnesty to give everyone a clear slate with the full knowledge that any professional snooker player caught gambling on snooker from that point will receive a life ban from the sport. Of course the clever ones will just get round it by getting their mates to place the bets for them; it's impossible to police really.

At least in 2010 we didn't have smartphones and betting apps for Alex to use – goodness knows what trouble he'd have got into; he was high maintenance enough without an iPhone.

While Alex Higgins was high maintenance, John Parrott was the easiest and most professional player I have ever worked with. It's well documented that JP was not on my original list of legends. I wanted Ray Reardon, but I am so glad we got him on board. Legends is a mix of the guys who are there to pot the balls – Jimmy, Ronnie, Stephen Hendry – and those who are there much more for entertainment and nostalgia: Dennis Taylor, Thorburn, Davis, and of course John Virgo.

In 2010 JP fell into both these categories: at the time we booked him he was still playing on the tour but he was a natural entertainer – hence his nickname, 'The Entertainer'. John has this great ability to make anyone he talks to feel special. Nothing is too much trouble and he takes every job he does very seriously.

In the first year of the tour it became pretty competitive between him and Jimmy; at that time we ran a format that provided one winner each night. They probably won 85 per cent of the nights, with Dennis picking up the rest. Cliff didn't win a night until the end of the tour, and boy did we all party that night!

I noticed that although the nights remained largely exhibition, Jimmy and JP were arriving early each day to make sure they got some time on the table before play. Pressure was being exerted on my table fitters to get the table up earlier and earlier.

The Crucible night is always remembered and documented as being the last time Alex Higgins ever played snooker. What people don't know is that it was also the night that convinced John Parrott to retire from the tour.

When I booked him he was also working for the BBC horse-racing team and was covering the Grand National at Aintree the day of our launch show. This meant a mad dash after the last race across the M62 to get to Sheffield for Legends. Our VIP reception began at 6pm.

The VIP reception was something I introduced to give the fans a chance to get up close to the players. Of course they paid a premium price, but they got a glass of champagne and a prime seat as well – plus they got to spend half an hour in the reception with the players so they could get autographs, photos, etc.

The VIP hospitality experience has been well received by all our fans. World Snooker never offered this at any of their events in 2010 – they do now! I also brought in autograph signings after the show so that although people with standard tickets couldn't enjoy the champagne reception, or the best seats, if they were happy to queue after the matches, each of them could get a handshake and autograph from every one of the legends appearing that night. Again this has proved very popular with the fans.

It's a fact that by 2015 the signings had become so popular on our Ronnie shows that we had to stop doing them. I remember a show in Poole in Dorset where the queue stretched for almost two hours after the match had finished. I wouldn't have minded if it was because all 1,600 people had wanted to buy something, but the truth was they all just wanted a 'selfie'. We were finishing at midnight, which was unacceptable for everyone.

JP turned up in Sheffield that first night and had to queue to get into the car park. He later was quoted as thinking, 'What the hell is going on in Sheffield tonight?' He had no idea the gridlock was being caused by the Legends show, and of course Alex's return.

Cliff Thorburn landed in the UK two days before the show and stayed at a hotel close to my house in Essex. My home had a snooker room and so it was ideal for practice. Cliff became a regular visitor to my home; when the son of the partner I had at the time used to tell people a famous snooker star was at his house every day, I'm sure they didn't believe him. It certainly gave him a good 'show and tell' subject in his class.

Cliff is one of my best friends in snooker, I'd never have thought that as a child, although Jimmy and Ronnie come a very close second. I had to court him a fair amount; living back in Canada he'd been out of the game for some time and was particularly bitter about having been forgotten by World Snooker. Between 2010 and 2016, they did stage the World Seniors Championship on Sky but in a format Barry wanted; it wasn't the right vehicle for Cliff or the other guys who had graced the game and helped build it. Cliff and Dennis were both in their mid sixties. The event they staged had them competing against Mark Williams who was just 39 and and recently became the World Professional Champion. There is a danger that with the current tables, and pitching them against professionals playing full-time 50 weeks a year, you make these guys look silly and that's not fair.

Dennis and Cliff have both made centuries on the Legends Tour, they've also both beaten Ronnie O'Sullivan over single frame matches: the pockets are the same size for both players. Would they beat him over best of five, best of nine? Maybe not, but in Legends they will never be exposed to that sort of risk. Why would anyone want to diminish in any way what these guys achieved?

By March 2010 Jimmy was sharing my concerns about Alex's health. I'd been sending food parcels to Belfast, and high-calorie drinks. Alex said he was feeling stronger; he was like a boxer in training camp preparing for a fight. Except of course this time making the weight was about Alex putting it on, not cutting it. Jimmy wanted Kevin to take him into his house in Cork for a month to build him up. There was access to a table for practice but no bookies! Kevin was reluctant; Jimmy couldn't see the problem and thought it was the least Kevin could do – then again it wasn't Jimmy who was being asked to deal with the Hurricane for a month. I'm not sure I'd have managed it. Kevin never entertained it.

On 5th April I got the call. Alex was in hospital with pneumonia – it was bad.

Jimmy was panicking; no one could provide an update. No one's calls were being answered. Jimmy eventually got through to Alex's sister Anne – Alex was weak and was looking at being at least a week in hospital. Well that's it, I thought, better to get him better for the next 17 dates even if it means we have to replace him in Sheffield.

Jimmy spoke to Ken Doherty. He was playing in the qualifiers for the World Championship at the Institute of Sport that same week, so was going to be nearby. He was also a former world champion, but he wasn't Alex. No one was Alex.

On 7th April Jimmy spoke to Jean, one of Alex's other sisters; there was no medical improvement but there was a resolve from him to be in Sheffield. Anne and Jean were adamant, as were the medical staff: Alex was in no fit state to leave hospital, let alone get on a plane and appear in a snooker exhibition. His weight was down to six stone. I didn't know what to do. We were deflecting press enquiries, not because we were trying to be evasive but because we simply didn't know.

At about 8pm on the 6th, just two days before the event itself, my phone went. 'Alex Higgins Mob' flashed up; it was the Hurricane himself. 'Get me a flight tomorrow lunchtime from Belfast City into Doncaster and tell no one, it's a better story. It's gonna cost me 600 euros to bribe a doctor to get me out of here, have the cash.' The phone went dead.

I was speechless.

I travelled north on the 7th with Cliff. I was still not sure Alex would make the plane but I'd booked the flight as asked and texted him the reference number so he could get his boarding pass. Alex hadn't replied. Cliff was on edge; there was 30 years of dislike between himself and Alex, but he also realised how important the Hurricane was for ticket sales.

The journey off the M1 into Sheffield was a welcome distraction. Cliff was sharing stories of past journeys to the championship, and the fact that he was about to play once more at the home of snooker was finally sinking in. Bear in mind this guy had done a 3,500-mile air trip just for one event – he wouldn't have been doing that for a night in Lewisham, trust me! Also, if you remember, in 1983 he stayed on to play the world final against Steve Davis having just been told that his wife Barbara had miscarried their baby. Sheffield had both good and bad memories for 'The Grinder'.

At 5pm I got the news that Alex had made the plane. Against all the odds Higgins was coming home to Sheffield.

I was in the foyer of the hotel with Cliff when he arrived. If anything he looked better than when I'd seen him in Dublin many months earlier.

Cliff and Alex made eye contact. It was tense but a respectful handshake took place… and the obligatory pint of Guinness was ordered. Far from being worried about him already requesting the 'black gold', I actually thought the iron in the stout would be beneficial to his immune system. Selfishly I had to do whatever I could to get him through the next 24 hours.

Alex's arrival had caused a stir. Many of the event team came out to witness the arrival of the legend, and with it his legendary reputation.

He took me to a quiet corner, more, I think, so I'd be able to hear him properly. I got the spiel about the 600 euros for the doctor's release. It was pointless arguing it but Alex had a new plan, and it was a beauty if we could make it happen.

Back in 1982, when Alex won the World Championship, the iconic image was one of him holding the Joe Davis trophy in one hand and clutching his daughter Lauren in the other. I doubt there is a snooker player over 40 who hasn't at some point seen that photo. The emotional scenes following his 18-15 victory over Ray Reardon where he called for his baby are some of the most replayed moments in snooker history.

Nowadays, it's almost a requirement that following a victory in a major tournament the winner's children and partner are wheeled out for the 'money shot' photo with the trophy. In 1982 this was not the norm; Alex once again paved the way for the scenes you see today of Ronnie and his little ones climbing all over the table being showered in confetti, or Mark Selby and his daughter Sofia kissing Daddy.

Alex's idea was to get Lauren down to Sheffield, and recreate the photo on the same spot in the Crucible, some 28 years on. He thought the tabloids would pay him £2,000 for the photo. No cut to me was mentioned but I immediately got tasked with phoning the red tops.

The *Daily Mirror* wanted it, but only for £500. Alex grabbed the phone to hurl abuse and try to settle on £1,000. The problem was his voice no longer carried the authority or caused the fear that it once did.

After an hour we'd agreed on £850 with the *Mirror*, in cash, but then Alex called off the deal after saying Lauren had to go to a job interview instead. I'm not even sure he spoke to her, or indeed that they were even speaking to each other at that time. The *Mirror* carried a snippet the next day saying the great Alex Higgins had come out of hospital and was in Sheffield for the Legends Night – I'm not sure getting a few headlines wasn't his plan all along.

I got Alex sorted with room service. I think it was a cottage pie that would be soft to digest, followed by ice cream... plus some medicinal Guinness of course.

With everything going on with Alex, Jimmy had decided not to travel till the next day. I think he knew it was going to be a circus and didn't want any part of it until the last possible moment. I later found out he was in Sheffield that night, booked into another hotel up the road. If anything I understood the need for the Whirlwind to stay away. Going back to the place that broke his heart on so many occasions was painful for him, and he had his own demons to face without getting involved in the Alex show.

My head hit the pillow. I had the Hurricane safely tucked up in the room next door, but what sort of storm he was going to cause the next day was anyone's guess.

CHAPTER 6

THE CRUCIBLE THEATRE, SHEFFIELD

8th April 2010

So the day had finally come. Months of planning and preparation and now we actually had to do this show.

All the players had agreed to have a chat with the BBC during the afternoon, everyone except Alex of course! These interviews formed a series of mid-session special features during the main 2010 World Championship. It was tremendous free promotion for the brand. The feature they did on Alex involved older footage with a few shots of him playing on the night and some sound bites from the other players. The irony is I think the BBC would have paid him for an interview, but for once he never even asked.

As part of my notion of recreating the iconic moments from past victories, Alex had agreed to wear a bottle-green shirt and to come on wearing his fedora hat, just as he had in 1982. We had arranged a photocall at 5.30pm, with the VIP reception due to start at 6. The day had flown by. It was the first time we had set up the event and we were finding our feet.

At 5pm we had finished the set-up. I was pretty proud of how it looked. We had transformed the Crucible and taken it back 30 years to the Embassy era of red carpets and gold trim. Kevin showed up in his tuxedo having done fuck all, all day. Co-promoter, my arse!

Jimmy had already arrived and was having a knock on the table, soaking up the venue that had been the scene of such emotion for him. Kevin had bad news: Alex wanted his money now and he wanted an extra £500 on top.

I was fuming. He had me over a barrel and the truth is, I would have paid it.

Jimmy stepped in and said, 'If you do it this time, you'll have this every time we play – tell him to fuck off and that you're calling Doherty to come and replace him.'

It was not his business to get involved but I think he genuinely felt sorry that Higgins was trying to screw me over at this late stage. I relayed the message to Kevin who was sent scuttling back to the Jurys Inn in his evening suit to pass on the news.

Jimmy reassured me Alex would play. I had the one thing no one had ever been able to offer him since 1994: a chance to play in the Crucible. He was right.

Five-thirty came and we all assembled at the table for the photo, all except Alex, who was still in his dressing room. Like a lap dog I went to get him after being told he wasn't ready. I opened the door, and he was sat fully dressed with his feet up, looking at the *Racing Post* – of course he was ready, but it was their place to wait for him. The green shirt didn't fit but Alex didn't want to roll up his cuffs – once again I'd soon realise why, the clever bugger.

Photos were done. Little did I know how many times that image would be used globally over the coming months.

It was 8th April 2010, and in just nine weeks Alex Higgins would be dead.

The format for the evening pitched two players into semi-finals in the first half, with John Virgo doing some trick shots and impressions. The second half would be a fun doubles with two members of the audience partnering the losing semi-finalists, before the final of the event itself to decide who would win the Legends Cup.

The initial match-ups were easy; Jimmy and John Parrott would recreate their 1991 final as a warm-up to the main event, a rematch between sworn enemies Thorburn and Higgins from 1980.

In the 1980 World Championship the top eight seeds didn't play in round one. Thorburn was seeded three and defeated Doug Mountjoy, Jim Wych and David Taylor to get to his second final, the first having been a 1977 loss to John Spencer.

Alex had to play from the first round and had beaten Tony Meo, Perrie Mans, arch-rival Steve Davis, and Kirk Stevens. It was a final between two bitter rivals, but Alex thought it was destined to be his year and started showboating, playing extravagant shots; he led 9-5 overnight. Apparently that evening Alex placed an order for a celebration cake, to be inscribed 'Alex Higgins 1980 World Champion'. Day two and Thorburn came out firing; he tightened up his game and clawed back the deficit.

During the final session these two gladiators went blow for blow, but unbeknown to them, a few hundred miles down the road in London, real hand grenades were being thrown and people's lives were being lost.

As famously reported, the coverage of the 1980 snooker final was interrupted by reports of a siege in London. The BBC took the snooker off the air to bring live coverage of the SAS storming the Iranian Embassy in Kensington. A group of six armed men had stormed it a few days earlier and taken 26 people hostage. The hostage-takers demanded the release of Arab prisoners from jails in the Khūzestān Province and their own safe passage out of the United Kingdom. The British government were not going to give in to their demands, and after one of the hostages was murdered, the SAS were sent in to resolve the situation.

This was a worldwide act of terrorism but as soon as the

BBC switched off the snooker to start reporting it, they were bombarded by the public demanding Alex and Cliff be put back on. Can you imagine that nowadays? 'Sorry, we have to leave coverage of the London bombings because Mark Selby and Shaun Murphy are into a decider'?

A compromise was reached, with the coverage switching between the two events. It's even been reported, although not verified as far as I know, that Margaret Thatcher had a TV set on following the snooker as well!

In 1980 Thorburn was the underdog, Higgins the people's champion. By 2010 not even the most fanatic of Alex's disciples would have bet on him to beat Cliff.

What was amazing was when Alex got his moment, walking into a packed arena on the back of a huge build-up from John Virgo. Nine hundred and ninety-seven people stood up and applauded, thanking Alex for what he had done for the game of snooker. He was back home for the first time since 1994. What followed was largely irrelevant – they had seen their man and, as we now know, they were affectively saying goodbye.

Alex was playing with the hybrid cue, top half Jimmy Mansfield's and bottom half from God knows where. He had cut the thumb from some bright yellow marigold gloves and stretched it over the butt of the cue to give him some sort of tactile grip – it was very bizarre.

The cuffs were now rolled up. Why? Well, because on his right wrist, in full view of the cameras, was Alex's hospital admission band – he never missed a trick!

Over the years I've been criticised for allowing Alex to play that night. Some said the whole thing was a freak show and I was exploiting him just for ticket sales. If you had never met, or been around, Alex then maybe I could understand you having that opinion. If on the other hand you had ever had anything on any level to do with him then you would know that *no one* told Alex what to do. He checked himself out of hospital, travelled to Sheffield and played that night because he wanted to do it.

Could I have stopped him? I could have tried, but who was I to deny a man who had done so much to get to the venue the chance to play in it? More recently I've got to know Lauren Higgins, his only daughter. She's lived her life being 'that baby in his arms' during the trophy celebrations. Now in her late thirties she's carved her own career, finally emerging from her father's shadow. She only rarely gives interviews about him despite being constantly asked. She did agree to present the first ever Alex Higgins trophy in Belfast in 2016; it was a nice touch and appreciated by the eventual winner Mark King.

We recently also welcomed the most famous Northern Irish snooker name ever back to the Legends family, with Lauren joining us in Goffs for the Irish Masters in January 2018. Davis, White, Taylor and Higgins all together again at the venue where Alex first courted Lauren's mum Lynne.

Alex Higgins was a trailblazer to many subsequent professional snooker players, including Ken Doherty, Jimmy White and Ronnie O'Sullivan. Ronnie is on record as saying that 'Alex was an inspiration to thousands of snooker players all over the country, including me. The way he played at his best is the way I believe the game should be played. It was on the edge, keeping the crowd entertained and glued to the action.'

He'd made the effort to get to Sheffield and he wanted to play.

I'd mentioned to John Virgo about not just performing his trick shots but also giving some live commentary during the frames. I was always aware that we had to set ourselves apart from tournament snooker.

We couldn't compete with the standard being dished out by O'Sullivan, Robertson and Selby, but we also didn't have the restrictions that tournament snooker brings. Amid the deathly silence of match play, one rogue cough in the crowd on a player's backswing can cost them a title and a good few quid.

JV wasn't immediately sold on the idea but agreed to give it a go. When you have natural entertainers like Parrott, Taylor and Davis playing, then they fill in the gaps, with a joke here, and a story there. My issue was that if Jimmy wasn't potting balls and making big breaks, or Cliff was struggling and having an off-night – as they all do from time to time – then the show could become at best awkward but at worst embarrassing.

John Virgo provided the glue to hold it all together. What he did was perfect; it worked far better than I could ever imagine and has become a feature of all our Legends shows. John knows when to speak, and more importantly, when to keep quiet. If a frame goes messy he will be out at the table offering advice on a 'plant' or certain shots they should play. If O'Sullivan is on nine reds and nine blacks, with a maximum looming, you won't hear JV telling you about when Ray Reardon found a talking frog!

In his recently published autobiography, *Say Goodnight, JV*, I was humbled to receive a personal acknowledgement from him. He thanked me for 'giving him another lease of life touring with Snooker Legends and the laughs along the way'. Who knew, this first night, one of the most stressful ever, would be the start of something that would change the direction of my life forever.

In my players' contracts, in all honesty mainly because of Alex's reputation, I had inserted a clause banning alcohol from backstage. All these legends, save JP, had a penchant for enjoying a small libation and I was terrified they would get pissed and make a fool of themselves, and more importantly the event itself.

The clause was ignored: green room fridges were filled with Budweiser and Guinness and even the Grinder Cliff was demanding 'Two fingers of vodka and some tonic'. (I soon learned that 'two fingers' was the measure taken from the bottom of the glass.)

Barry had sent a few 'guests' along; I think they were friendly spies. Mike Ganley, his tournament director, spends his whole life running the snooker tournaments – why on earth he'd want to spend a day off sat in the very seats he managed for 17 days every year was baffling... unless of course he was reporting back!

The first half of the show went well. JP defeated Jimmy, another loss for Jimmy in the Crucible, and Cliff easily defeated Alex 2-0. I always thought JP and Jimmy was even money, but I wasn't surprised to see Cliff beat a very fragile Hurricane. I think a fit and healthy Alex would have been a bit embarrassed at how he played, barely putting up a fight; the outcome was to be the same as 1980 but nowhere near as close a battle.

During the 20-minute interval I was doing the rounds. The atmosphere was good, the show was working, but Jimmy was nowhere to be found... unless you were in the queue in the foyer lining up to buy his merchandise.

I was fuming. Snooker Legends had our own merchandise, including Jimmy photos he would be contractually required to sign. By sitting there chatting, he was devaluing every VIP package I had sold, which gave the people who paid top money their time with the players. You could argue why would you pay for a VIP package if one of the main stars was going to sit by his own 'shop' in the interval? It was pure greed.

I wasn't happy, and even though I didn't know Jimmy or Kevin that well, I let them both know it was unacceptable. It never happened again! I was struggling to make Jimmy see that this was not a two-bit exhibition in some back-arse club where you try and nick a few quid.

It didn't take Jimmy long to buy in to the Legends notion or ethos and it's one he now defends fiercely. Ironic really.

The rest of the evening went well; Michaela Tabb, the lady referee, had been a delight and was so good with the public. It still annoys me now when players are signing a piece of merchandise for a fan whilst looking the other way or having a third-party conversation. Jimmy can still be guilty of this whereas Michaela makes everyone she meets feel like a million dollars.

Alex remained fairly well behaved. People queued for ages to meet him afterwards, and he shook every hand and signed every photo. The plan was to go back to the Jurys Inn for a little reception and I thought I could finally relax.

Alex was still on about his £600 cash for the doctor; I knew I'd have to pay it from the merchandise sales. As with all these things, I got caught up at the venue for a while, sorting 'stuff', as you do, and didn't get back to the hotel for 45 minutes.

Higgins had gone off to bed screaming that he hadn't been paid and had been ripped off; no one else seemed to get caught up in his theatricals. I went up to the room with my colleague Nick to find a note punched across the door handle.

It started with the words 'Dear Jason' but after that the pleasantries ended; the version I can publish roughly translates into the fact he felt let down and ripped off. I knocked on the door and we were summoned in. Alex was in bed with what seemed like his life's possessions strewn all over it, all within arm's reach. 'Where's my money?' he rasped, venom in his eyes.

'It's here, Alex,' I said and went to give him the envelope containing £600.

'Put it on the bed, I'll be checking it.'

I welcomed him to check it and explained I had been caught up in packing up, that's why I was later getting back – not that I had set a time. It dawned on me that he wasn't actually pissed off with me but he was now in a place where he could exert some authority and be an arsehole, so it was my turn to be the innocent victim.

'I want more money next time and I'm only playing Jimmy. I want the money up front and I want someone with me at all times to look after me.'

I understood the request for more money – it probably irked him to see a full house and six people on the wage bill when even I couldn't argue he had filled most of the seats himself. He wanted more of the cake, and the only person getting crumbs would be the Whirlwind.

I explained that Kevin was supposed to be looking after him...

'Fuck that Irish c**t, you can do it.'

'Alex, you've signed a contract and agreed the money. I'm not paying you any more money, and I can't just have you playing Jimmy.'

Alex pulled back the covers and swung his legs over the side of the bed. Nick later said he thought he was going to come for me. The truth is he hardly had the strength to sit up.

'You pay me more money or I'm not playing.'

'Then don't play, Alex,' I said, I think overcome by tiredness and emotion of the day, and of course his unreasonable behaviour.

'Fuck off out of my room,' he said. 'More money or I ain't playing no more.'

I retreated to the door and then I realised deep down that this couldn't go on.

'Alex, I need to know if you are going to play the rest of the tour. I want you to be happy but not everything can revolve around you.'

The reply was genius.

'Listen, you c**t, everything does revolve around me... Now fuck off!'

I pulled the door closed but then reopened it. 'I'm sorry, Alex, but I'm not prepared to work like this. I won't be using you on the rest of this tour.'

'Fuck off!' he rasped and the *Sporting Life* was thrown in my direction, landing well short of the door but far enough from him to ensure that he was going to have to get up to retrieve it before he could place his next bet.

I returned downstairs. Nick was fully supportive, but I was in a daze. The party was in full flow, Jimmy and Cliff sharing old stories and JV into his third or fourth lager.

Michaela handed me a pint. We'd only met earlier that day but already I had a strange feeling we were to become great friends. Jimmy and JV came over for a chat.

'Brilliant night, Jay,' said Jimmy.

'Superb,' added JV, 'and a great idea to do the live commentary.'

'We can do hundreds of these,' said Jimmy. 'All we gotta do is find a way to control him [meaning Alex] and get him better.'

'Yeah, Alex is the key,' said JV.

Little did they know I'd already sacked him, and although we'd speak again on the phone, that was the last time I'd ever see the Hurricane.

CHAPTER 7

AFTER ALEX... AND THAT NIGHT IN BLACKBURN

The tour made national news and elevated Snooker Legends into the snooker public's eye, but with just one show done I already had a PR disaster on my hands. The 'top of the bill' had been sacked and no one knew.

I'd broken the news to Virgo first; he thought I was mad and begged me to phone Alex. 'You know what he's like. Jimmy and I have had a lifetime of it. That's Alex.'

Jimmy asked if the tour was going to be cancelled!

Cliff knew it was the right decision. Alex had already been such a disruptive influence that to think the next 17 shows would go off without there being a major incident between those two, or Alex and any of the team in general, was unrealistic. Ticket sales were going well; what was called for was a strategy of damage limitation.

I'd decided not to take JV's advice to ring Alex and got Cliff to speak with Dennis Taylor instead. Dennis was Cliff's best friend on tour and the Grinder thought he would fit in perfectly. He was a former world champion, so no one could argue he wasn't a legend, and he'd played in the most-watched snooker final in history in 1985. He was also another member of the BBC commentary team, which was key. In that first year the tour was advertised live on-air, during matches he was commentating on, literally dozens of times. I don't think you could overestimate how valuable this was. It was certainly something we could never have funded. I got away with it for two years before the BBC clamped down. It was getting comical, with fans forecasting how many times Dennis would mention the Legends Tour during his broadcasts – good fella!

Dennis said he would love to join the tour but had a clash on a few of the dates so I'd need to cover them. I was still in turmoil. Interview requests were still coming in for Alex, and I was aware people were buying tickets to see him play. I knew we were misleading them. I knew the next morning I had to speak to the venues and issue a press release.

At about 9pm that night my phone flashed. It was the Hurricane.

'Jason, it's Alex. How much was in that envelope?'

'It was £600, Alex, as agreed.'

'I didn't count it but I think someone stole some of it from me.'

Awkward silence.

'I'm not well, and don't think I can continue on the tour.'

My head spun. What? Just three days ago I sacked you – what are you on about? I thought.

'Alex, I've already spoken to Dennis Taylor about doing the rest of the tour in your place.'

'He won't sell you any tickets. You need me but I'm not well enough.'

I knew what he was doing: I still owed him £500 for an autograph session he did for me before Sheffield so we could make up some memorabilia. The deal was he would get paid when it was sold.

'I'll let you know when I'm well enough and we'll do some

more, but just me, Jimmy and John Virgo, and the referee is OK as well.'

This was a very different Alex from the one who'd screamed at me in Sheffield. I agreed to issue a statement saying he was not well enough to continue the tour. I wouldn't mention I sacked him and he agreed not to say anything bad about Snooker Legends... Oh and I was to send the £500 to him the next morning, first class of course.

This was the last time I would ever speak to him. We parted on OK terms and he did concede it was good to play again in Sheffield, but said his 'tip' had meant he couldn't play properly. If that is what he wanted to believe then so it was.

Pictures of him turned up in a newspaper a few weeks later in Marbella where someone had raised some money for him to get his teeth sorted. Amazingly he was wearing the same bottle-green shirt I'd given him in Sheffield: it must have been 100 degrees in the Spanish sun and here he was, the Hurricane in long sleeves. The reality was, I think, at the time it was probably the best shirt he owned.

No one was surprised when we announced his withdrawal from the tour. Dennis was on board, and Jimmy got on the phone and sorted Ken Doherty and Mark Williams to do the dates he couldn't.

By the time we got to Telford some three weeks later, everything had settled down. I was quickly losing patience with my so-called 'co-promoter' Kevin, and also now that I didn't have to deal with Alex, and had the personal contact with Jimmy, Kevin had very little left to offer the tour any more. He earned a few quid from the Crucible date, enough to buy his polytunnel to grow his organic veg in Cork! We never fell out, and I see quite a bit of him now at events, but he had no place in the management or promotion of the tour any more.

At our second show the Legends Tour really took shape. It was still a night of snooker, but now we added the entertainment. The tension was gone and Dennis fitted in perfectly. Jimmy seemed more relaxed, and there was no sign of his personal merchandise stall. We laughed all night.

After Telford we went to places like Brentwood, Llanelli, Cardiff and Hoddesdon. A great night followed at the Assembly Rooms in Derby but by the time we got to King George's Hall in Blackburn on 28th May we had another reason to celebrate: it was Dennis Taylor's birthday!

During his professional career Dennis had based himself in and around the Blackburn area. People often report his famous fall-out with Alex Higgins when Alex threatened to have him 'shot'. They don't report that when Alex first came over to the UK it was Dennis who got him a flat in Blackburn and set him up with a TV set and a few quid spending money.

Alex once claimed that they fell out because Dennis fancied one of his sisters. The truth was the other way round, and Dennis has always refused to repeat what Alex said to him that caused the rift.

Dennis was the good guy from Belfast, Alex was the bad boy, and everyone loves the bad boy. Dennis didn't try to compete.

He'd created his own piece of history in 1985 when he beat Steve Davis to win the world title. To this day, that final achieved the highest ratings ever on BBC2, over 18 million. With his trademark 'upside down' glasses he developed his own character and he was a natural performer, perfect for Legends.

All the players on the tour claimed they never practise much. Utter rubbish. I don't think Ricky Walden's table in Chester was ever busier than during that first Legends season. Dennis was certainly putting the hours in; he hadn't played properly for eight years before the Legends Tour. Trust me, he can still play the game and was the only one to take a frame off Davis in 2018 when we staged their last-ever tournament match in Goffs.

Blackburn was a party atmosphere. As well as Dennis' family we also welcomed John Parrott's, the venue not being far from his home in Formby. Both of them were keen to impress, but they were drawn to play each other that night.

JP went on against Dennis and never got a shot. We all felt for him, but Dennis made 90 in the first frame and a century in the next. The trademark wagging finger and cue above the head were on show and the crowd loved it. JP was disappointed for his family. 'At least you've got the doubles [that same night],' I said. 'Make a few in that.'

The truth was the players weren't fond of the doubles; it's not so bad if you've got a competition winner as a partner, who plays a bit, but generally you get two random winners in the raffle and some of them have never held a cue before. Also of course there is no value in just seeing the legend clear the balls up; these winners deserve to enjoy playing on a world-class table with a cue they've just won and the experience of partnering a famous player.

Sadly for JP two things were flowing freely that night: the first was Dennis' cue arm and the second was the alcohol that the first raffle winner had consumed, the guy who got to partner him!

The guy wasn't short on confidence, or Guinness it seemed, and made a complete prat of himself. He basically ruined the frame. One minute he was grabbing Michaela, the next tapping the back of the pro's cue, a pet hate, and generally getting all cocky.

We all felt so bad for John. His family had come to watch him and he didn't get any chance to perform for them. Cliff was the other pro in the doubles and he seemed completely bemused by it all.

The final saw the 'birthday boy' take on the Whirlwind, a one-frame shoot-out. Destiny had already decided that tonight's event was only going one way. Dennis made another 80 and only just missed out on his second century. He had won in front of his family – it was time to party!

Whenever we stay away the standard of hotel is always variable. If I can get a reasonable deal we'll stay somewhere really nice; if not it's a Premier Inn with a continental breakfast.

In Blackburn I'd done a deal with the Mercure, a stunning country hotel, and we settled into our own little residents' bar to celebrate the champ's birthday and Legends win. Dennis had his son there, Damian, and the mood was good. The sandwiches and drinks arrived. There were a lot more drinks than sandwiches; everyone was having a good drink.

Out of nowhere JV stood up and started a sing-song. Well, that was it. He took us through his repertoire of Roy Orbison and the Beatles and soon it became almost like 'spin the bottle' when the next person had to get up and start a number then we all joined in.

We were all slaughtered come 2am. Cliff and Dennis had performed 'Up on the Roof' by The Drifters and even I'd had to belt out a bit of Elton John.

The few other residents in the hotel didn't really know what had hit them; one particular hippy couple were especially confused by it all, not having a clue who any of these guys were. It was like a remake of the film *Cocoon* in there with the old boys jiving.

I don't remember what time we got to bed; all I know was it was light outside and I wasn't the last to go.

Cliff was booked to appear at a Memorabilia fair the next day to sign autographs with Ray Reardon... in Milton Keynes, oh dear.

We'd agreed to get on the road at 8am. Thankfully someone else was driving. I was hanging bad and as for Cliff... well, in his own words, 'it wasn't pretty'.

The trip south was about two hours but Cliff hadn't even showered. About 20 minutes outside the MK National Bowl we pulled into a service station and Cliff threw some cold water over his face and brushed the moustache. He called the promoters to say he was going to be late and we'd had traffic. That would have been OK if the promoters themselves hadn't come down exactly the same road only an hour earlier!

With a packet of Extra Strong Mints Cliff started work. Ray of course had arrived early and was looking immaculate, despite his 77 years! Cliff felt really embarrassed.

I used the opportunity to try and 'tap up' Ray to guest at our Plymouth Show in July. He was one legend I desperately wanted to work with, but 'Dracula', as he was known in his playing days, was not overly keen.

I left Cliff and the six-time world champion surrounded by Klingons, Trekkies and some bloke from the *Twilight* film. We were off to Ireland in a few days and I needed a break, and some aspirin.

On the morning of the flights to Ireland I got a call to say JV had been taken ill. It was another panic. Luckily Ken Doherty was able to cover the two shows and Dennis took over the commentary job and trick shots. Team.

Killarney was disappointing sales-wise but Citywest in Dublin did well. It was on the flight between Kerry and Dublin that I first had the idea of the Legends Cup. I'd visited the K Club and The Belfry as a fan to watch golf's Ryder Cup and I always thought something in snooker could work the same way.

By now JP, Dennis and Cliff had become a firm unit. They ate together, played golf together and laughed a lot. I mean a lot. Both Dennis and Cliff are hilarious in their own ways and JP laughs at anything. It was lovely seeing them have so much fun together. Jimmy always kept himself a little bit separate from them, sticking mostly with JV.

I'd noticed that JV's neck injury was becoming a problem. He wasn't able to straighten his head, so he couldn't get down over the cue to play a shot.

A regret I have is that JV has never been well enough to play at a Legends event because I have never met a man who loves the game of snooker more than John. Because he has been the lead commentator for so long with the BBC, people forget just how good a player he was, winning the UK Championship and reaching the semi-final of the World's. In his amateur days I'm also told he was a fearsome money match player in the Salford area, as was Patsy Fagan, a legend I've come to know and also employ at a few shows.

On 15th July 2010 it finally happened – Cliff won! He beat Jimmy in the final. It was a huge relief for him and boy did he lap it up. Everyone was delighted for him and all the event girls wore the Cliff-range T-shirt in the hotel afterwards, posing for photos like they were his Charlie's Angels.

The tour finished in Doncaster. There was general sadness that it was over, but for once it was the team's turn to surprise me. Unbeknown to me they had smuggled my own cue up and when we came to announce the doubles match, John Virgo announced that I was partnering Cliff. I truly had no idea.

I was still in shock when Michaela presented me with my cue; it was my turn to play in front of a Legends crowd. I think Cliff broke and the other raffle winner played a shot. I got in and made about a dozen, I think. JV was giving me some stick and even Jimmy was out watching. I played a safety and JP screamed one in. He made a century and I never got another shot – that's snooker for you! It was a tremendous gesture by the team and they also presented me with a signed photo from them all.

Without discussing it with the players I announced over the microphone that we'd be doing a 2011 tour. I had no doubt we were all in this for the long term.

CHAPTER 8

THE BUDWEISER MAXIMUM

May 2010

For one of our nights we arrived in Redhill, Surrey for what was to be anything but a normal Legends event.

At the previous seven events the Legends Cup had been shared between Jimmy and John Parrott, apart from Cardiff where Mark Williams played and just made everyone look silly with two centuries in three frames. It was amazing how competitive they suddenly all became.

Cliff was struggling for form, adapting to the fast cloths and a tournament table again. Dennis had made his first Legends century and was playing well, but he wasn't beating JP or Jimmy. We rotated the match-ups and when Dennis faced Cliff, it was not one for the purists, that's for sure.

Redhill is in Surrey and Jimmy lives in Surrey, which meant I knew his requests for tickets might increase that night. With five kids, and more hangers than a dry cleaner's, I think I could have filled the venue that night just with his entourage.

The event had sold well and quickly the 10 tickets Jimmy needed became 20, then 25. We had nowhere to put them all but

I was expected to just create seats. I wasn't in the best of moods, plus he turned up with his partner's family and was already well into the bottled lagers by the time the VIP reception took place.

It was our seventh show in two weeks and everyone was tired. Michaela, our usual referee, was already booked elsewhere, so a less-experienced referee, Trish Murphy, was stepping in.

JV did his trick shots and lifted the crowd, and JP went on to play Dennis. Dennis threw an 80 break into him and won comfortably 2-0. During this time a further six bottles lay strewn backstage near to where Jimmy was supposed to be waiting to play!

Jimmy was the worse for wear when he went on to play Cliff. The first frame was awful; Cliff was struggling and Jimmy was tipsy – it wasn't really what people had paid for. More alcohol was appearing at the playing table, courtesy of one or more of the extended family who'd suddenly turned into table-service waiters – the mood was a little uneasy.

Jimmy took the first frame; JV was doing his best to keep everyone entertained. To say it was a struggle was an understatement. Into frame two.

After a safety exchange, Cliff missed a long shot and left Jimmy an easy red along the top rail. The Whirlwind dropped it in but was left low on the black; if he took it on he was certain to split the pack everywhere.

He smashed the black in at about 100mph and the table looked like someone had emptied a bowl of cherries all over it. More importantly he was plum on the next red, and the black went into both pockets. Soberness descended on the Whirlwind, expectation descended in the crowd.

By the time we got to ten reds and ten blacks you could hear a pin drop.

A maximum '147' break is a rare thing in snooker. Hendry and Ronnie hold the tournament record of 12 or 13 each I think, but that's in a career that has spanned over 20 years each and hundreds of tournaments. Twelve reds, then thirteen… it was on. Here was a man, who at a conservative guess must have had ten bottles of beer in him, on course to make the first ever Legends maximum. Trish was shaking more than Jimmy; she was closest to the action.

The fifteenth black went in. You could cut the atmosphere with a knife. Yellow, green, brown followed, tricky blue… it's in and we are on the pink. Deep screw off the side cushion required on the pink, never a gimme… Yes!

I didn't hear Trish say the words '147'. The crowd erupted and we got a bit of a pitch invasion as everyone congratulated Jimmy. He had done it.

We sat in the dressing room in the interval and the mood was amazing. Jimmy seemed sober; collectively everyone knew that this maximum gave the tour huge credibility. This was not just old farts knocking a few balls about; they could still perform!

After the doubles match Jimmy and Dennis were introduced for the one-frame final. Jimmy screamed a long red in, took the black and once more split the pack. By the time he had taken only the fourth red and black the murmur had already started…

There's another max on here, I thought to myself, barely able to comprehend what I was witnessing.

Already the only problem ball I could see was the pink; it was tight to the cushion. It was weird but I had no doubt in my mind that all the remaining 11 reds were going to be taken with blacks; Jimmy was hitting the ball so sweetly. There was a real chance we could see back-to-back maximums. The break reached 120, just the six colours for history.

Yellow, green, brown were dispatched no problem. Jimmy was going to need to use the angle on the blue to move the pink.

The blue crept in off the knuckle. It wasn't a clean contact by any means, but agonisingly the cue ball slipped past the pink. The crowd groaned, JV kept the faith.

'If any man can find this, Jimmy can,' whispered JV.

Jimmy's only hope was a double on the pink, it jawed and the break finished on 134 – we almost felt cheated!

Jimmy White was two balls away from creating snooker history, back-to-back maximums.

I left soon after the show. I don't think they celebrated with Budweisers: the bar was dry and the next dray delivery wasn't due till Tuesday!

CHAPTER 9

SNARING DRACULA

The 10th of July 2010 is another important date in Legends history. We were in Plymouth and Michaela announced words I'd been waiting a long time to hear: 'The first frame, Ray Reardon to break.'

'Dracula', as he is affectionately known, was always on my original list of legends for the first tour. Ray was very rarely seen any more, only occasionally popping up at the final of the World's as a sponsor's guest. I'd tracked him down via Churston Golf Club in Brixham, Devon, where he was the president.

He did contact me initially but felt that touring the country for 18 nights was too much at his age. However, he did eventually agree to be the special guest at our show at the Plymouth Pavilions after I met him in person with Cliff in Milton Keynes and wouldn't take no for an answer. The original date had to be moved because of a clash with a qualifier Jimmy had. 'No problem to me,' said Ray. 'I'm retired.'

He turned up at about 3pm, just the three hours early! He wanted to get used to the table. Two of his closest friends had driven him down. They told me that he was still making centuries in practice on the table at their golf club; they too were delighted to see him honoured in this way.

Jimmy, Cliff and the boys were genuinely excited and a little bit humbled to have Ray there – it was like the Godfather of the sport had arrived.

Ray was a different generation to the rest of the players on the tour. Only Cliff and Dennis were playing when he was at his peak winning titles – and they were just starting out.

Ray was from the coal mining community of Tredegar in Wales. Wanting to play snooker, he turned down a place at grammar school to become a miner at just 14, following in the footsteps of his father. After a rock fall, in which he was buried for three hours, he quit mining, moved his family to Stoke and became a police officer.

He won his first world title in 1970, the year I was born, beating John Pulman in the final 37-33; yes, the final was the best of 73, not 35 as it is today. It was played not at the Crucible in Sheffield but at London's Victoria Hall.

Between 1973 and 1976, Ray played 17 World Championship matches without defeat and won the title four years in a row. When the snooker world rankings were introduced in 1976, Ray was the first number one, retaining that position until 1981/1982. His sixth, and final, world title came in 1978 when he beat South African Perrie Mans, his only victory at the Crucible. Amazingly though, in 1982, despite being 49, he was still world number one. He remains the oldest player, at 50, ever to win a ranking tournament.

Everyone talks about the 1985 final when Dennis Taylor potted the final black to beat Steve Davis in front of 18.5 million viewers. People forget that the person 'The Nugget' beat in the semi-finals that year was Ray, who was 52 years old. I can't see anyone in the modern-day game getting close to repeating that feat, although the recent antics of a certain Mr O'Sullivan may prove me wrong.

Back to Plymouth, and it was time to get underway…

JV would always do some impressions at the start of the show. Ray wasn't due to appear until later but we hatched a plan where that night JV would do his 'Reardon' impression and pretend that Ray wouldn't know he was doing it, telling the audience he was in the dressing room.

We rigged a special light by the curtain and just as JV was doing the famous 'Reardon Shoulder Shake', the man himself popped his head round the curtain. It was staged but the audience didn't know that, and I don't think they cared. The place went mad.

The amazing thing about the people who attend these Legends nights is that they are all there for a reason. This is not the sort of event that's a tag-along, where reluctant relations feel they have to go – these are all snooker fans who are genuinely thrilled to see their heroes from yesteryear. I think Ray was shocked at the reception he got as well. The smile was beaming, even if the new shoes he had purchased to wear were pinching a little!

He played remarkably well, made quite a few decent balls and laughed a lot. The legends who weren't playing that frame usually stayed in the dressing room but they all came out to watch him. Here was an Honorary Legend, if there is such a thing.

While the boys enjoyed a beer Ray refused to have anything but tea until after the job was done. Finally, when we did the autographs, Jimmy got the first gin and tonic into him, and it was lovely to see him relax. I know Michaela especially loved having him around. I only wished he was 20 years younger as I know he would have been so well received on the Legends Tour.

On 10th July 2010 Ray Reardon played at Snooker Legends; on the same night, Alex Higgins died alone in his Belfast flat, he was only 61. It would be over a week until his sister Anne found him, a complete tragedy.

CHAPTER 10

RIP THE PEOPLE'S CHAMPION

I hadn't spoken to Alex since the middle of April; Jimmy had also had very little contact, save an appearance at an event in Manchester to raise money for his new teeth. I'd seen from the newspapers that he'd been in Marbella, but as the tour finished on 17th July we all went our separate ways, and Jimmy headed off to Thailand for the Six-Red World Championship.

I got a tip-off on 24th July from a radio presenter at BBC Belfast who I'd worked with a while back. The story was about to break that Alex Higgins had been found dead and they wanted to speak with Jimmy. I was the only contact they had. I begged them to give me some time to contact him. The last thing I wanted was to let Jimmy hear it on a TV in some bar or restaurant in Bangkok.

I felt numb. When someone passes and you've been a part of their life for such a short time, it's difficult to know what sort of emotion you should experience. Alex wasn't my friend; he was someone I'd worked with. In early 2010 I was someone he trusted for a while, but in fact I was the meal ticket for a few months, I know that. If I am honest, he treated me very badly, but I still had a duty to let those who were closest to him know that he had passed on. Plus, of course, he was still my playing hero and he was gone.

I phoned Jimmy. It went to answerphone. I asked him to call me urgently.

Then I called Ken Doherty. Ken had done a lot for Alex, including staging a sell-out show in 1997 at the Waterfront in Belfast to raise money for Alex shortly after Ken became world champion. He was with Joe Swail, another player, in Thailand. I asked if he was with Jimmy; he wasn't. I told him Alex was gone. He didn't show much emotion, stunned I think.

'OK,' he said, his voice hushed. 'We need to find Jimmy.'

I explained that the story was soon going to be all over the news so we didn't have long. With the media nowadays, news goes worldwide in a matter of minutes. The death of the 'The Hurricane' was big news.

At that moment my phone bleeped. Jimmy was ringing back. I took the call.

'Go on, son,' he said. That was how Jimmy always answered the phone. I asked where he was; he was walking back to his hotel from a restaurant. I asked if he was alone; he said he was. I took a deep breath.

'Sorry, mate, Alex has died.'

'When?' he replied.

'I just got a tip-off from the BBC in Belfast. The news is about to break but I wanted to make sure you knew first.'

'OK,' he said. 'Yeah, terrible news.'

Then, as he reports in his own book, Jimmy went on to talk about the match he had played that day. He was talking about a new shorter cue action he'd been trying, and we discussed how happy he was with his tip.

In some ways it may have seemed totally inappropriate to be chatting about his cue action at a time like this, but this is how

Jimmy was digesting the news that his best friend in snooker, his inspiration and his kindred soul, was gone.

I said I'd spoken to Ken and I'd let the rest of the boys know. I was worried about Jimmy: I knew there would be media requests, and they'd all be looking to speak with him.

'Take care of yourself,' I said.

After the call Jimmy sat on the pavement and cried for 30 minutes… alone. He cut short his plans and travelled back to the UK.

I had to deliver the news to Dennis, Cliff and JP. By the time I got to Virgo, he already knew.

Aside from Jimmy, JV was Alex's best friend in the sport. Bear in mind that during some of that time John was on the board of the WPBSA, the very body that was having to deal with the unruly Higgins. Their friendship prevailed despite all those fines and suspensions.

John would tell stories about Alex, like the time when they visited India for a tournament in 1979 and Alex, drunk, caused a huge diplomatic incident by groping a dignitary. Such was the seriousness of his actions that the players were told that they would not be allowed to leave the country until Alex had written an apology. Alex duly delivered the apology… written on toilet paper!

Alex got away with it; he always got away with it.

The truth is he affected the lives of so many people and yet in the latter years so many of those people turned their backs on him. Cliff once said Alex could cause an argument with himself in a lift – I knew what he meant.

My own opinion, for what it's worth, is that Alex was angry and bitter for the way the people within World Snooker had treated him and he carried that anger, and took it out, on people 20 years on who really didn't deserve it. So many people tried to help him but he fucked them all off. No one will ever question Alex's ability, and what he did for snooker – plus he beat cancer. Don't forget or underestimate that.

Back in the 1980s World Snooker struggled to control their most-prized commodity. (I'd say that with Ronnie O'Sullivan, modern-day snooker has a similar quandary.) In 1980 Alex was still able to charge twice as much as Cliff Thorburn for an exhibition, the man who had just been crowned world champion by beating him.

The general consensus is that the people within the game of snooker could have helped him more. The Authorities at the time made an example of him to try to control him. If two players got fined for the same offence, and one of those players was Alex, then the perception was the Hurricane always got hit harder.

When Jimmy is asked about Alex he says he is angry, angry that Alex wouldn't help himself. But also this is the 21st century; should someone of his stature be allowed to die of malnutrition?

In the ITV4 life story documentary that was made on Jimmy in 2013 he called the fact Alex perished this way a 'fucking liberty' – it's difficult to argue.

I didn't travel to Belfast for Alex's funeral; I felt it would have been fake. I'd known him personally for no more than six months. It was time for Jimmy, Alex's family, and players like Ken to say their farewells.

I felt almost embarrassed when a guy called Will Robinson started doing interviews and getting involved with organising the funeral, speaking as if he was his best friend.

Will had done some driving for him 20 years before. Suddenly Will had Alex's great niece, also called Alex, in a recording studio cutting a record and promoting it around the Hurricane's name. It all felt a bit unsavoury and was certainly not done with the knowledge, or blessing, of Alex's children – Lauren and son Jordan. He popped up again in the documentary the BBC did: while legends like Reardon, Davis, Ronnie, Barry and of course Jimmy were paying their tributes, so was Will. People were asking, 'Who is this fella?'

Will did organise the Chinese meal in Manchester to raise

money for Alex to get his teeth done. Jimmy went, and so did JV and Tony Knowles. It was billed as a night to raise money for a sporting hero who had fallen on hard times. As guests who had paid good money for this dinner queued to get into the restaurant, they saw Alex leaving the bookies opposite having got his bets on for the evening races!

The Snooker Legends Tour organised a floral tribute; it was in the shape of a triangle of 15 red roses. All the legends were meant to pitch in; it was about £300. I paid it up front and no one ever gave me a penny towards it.

On the day of the funeral itself I was in Spain on a family holiday. I was thrilled the people of Belfast came out on the streets to show their appreciation. His coffin was carried in a horse-drawn carriage. Ken joked that Alex had probably backed one of them in the past.

In 2011 the Legends Tour came to Belfast and we did it as an 'Alex Higgins Tribute Night'. I gave his sisters about 50 tickets and asked Jean and Anne to present the trophy.

Ken was playing, as was Jimmy. We cut together a montage of old photos and footage and put them with a song that had been written by a fan called Joe McNally. It was very touching and it was good to meet the sisters. Now that I've met, and got to know, Lauren Higgins I realise I should have invited her too. I did make up for that one in January 2018 when she came as my guest to the Senior Irish Masters in Goffs; she presented the trophy and met all the fans who shared a story or memory of her dad. Steve Davis won that event in his last ever appearance in Goffs, so it was fitting at the last knocking it was Davis and Higgins once more sharing centre stage.

It was sad when I spoke with Jean just after the show and she told me that there were still funeral costs left outstanding to pay. At the time of Alex's death everyone came out of the woodwork and got 'busy'. People who hardly knew him claimed to be as close as family.

Closing the streets of Belfast and horse-drawn carriages don't come cheap, but when it came to picking up the tab those so-called 'friends' had moved on. The whole event was managed on emotion not a spreadsheet, but the bill still had to be paid.

People always say you should never meet your heroes – I do know what they mean but I don't regret meeting Alex, and I'm proud that Snooker Legends gave him one final chance to go back and play in the Crucible.

CHAPTER 11

THE MAN IN THE WHITE SUIT

The 2011 tour kicked off in Guernsey and instead of 18 dates I'd booked 28. We had some momentum going and I wanted to capitalise on it. We were adding 19 new venues and revisiting the ones we had done good business at the previous year.

The main squad of players was going to be the same – Jimmy, JP, Cliff and Dennis – with JV and Michaela – but after the success of having Ray guest in Plymouth I decided that we should try to bring in some more legends for one-off events. My guest for the Crucible date in April was one that no one saw coming – 'The Man in the White Suit' was returning.

When people review historic moments in snooker they are usually taken from the finals of tournaments, or one-off moments like Ronnie's maximum in five minutes, twenty seconds against 'The Postman' Mick Price. There are, however, two matches that buck this trend and always get brought up amongst snooker fans when such discussions take place.

I don't think anyone would argue that the most famous match that wasn't a final was the 1982 World Championship semi-final between Alex and Jimmy. A young, unseeded Jimmy led 15-14, on the brink of his first world final. With just one frame required to beat his hero he got in first and was 59 points ahead. With balls all over the table, a clearance seemed unlikely, if not impossible. History shows that Alex made the finest 69 clearance the game has ever seen. He was hardly ever in prime position and just kept pulling out recovery pots under the intense pressure of knowing that one miss would hand the match to Jimmy. Alex not only defied logic to clear the balls but won the deciding frame to take the match 16-15. He consoled his young 'apprentice' in his arms, amidst his own muted celebrations.

The other match purists point to, and one that gets replayed a lot, is the 1984 Masters semi-final, between Jimmy and the man I'd just booked to come back for the 2011 Crucible Show, Canada's Kirk Stevens.

Kirk epitomised everything that was good and bad about 1980's snooker. He had the rock-star looks, a host of celebrity friends, beautiful women hanging off each arm... and a severe cocaine habit that almost killed him.

When modern-day players complain about having to travel overseas to China for three weeks, Cliff Thorburn is quick to point out that in the 1980s Kirk, Bill Werbeniuk and himself had to move their entire lives to the UK to play professional snooker. Those guys, and players like Eddie Charlton, were lucky if they got to spend three weeks at home a year. No one made special provisions for them.

Cliff handled it best of all; Bill turned to drink, often having five or six pints before a match to 'settle him down'. As for Kirk, he was the youngest of the players, miles from home and thrown into the celebrity spotlight when snooker was at its peak. There are urban myths about parties thrown by the late Freddie Mercury of rock band Queen where dwarves carried the cocaine in on silver platters. It was no myth: Kirk was a guest on many of these nights – sleep and rest were overrated, and the 'high' from using cocaine meant he could stay up for days on end.

I knew trying to get Kirk was a risk. He was two years into his latest effort to keep clean, and although it was working, travelling away from the trusted support network that had got him this far could jeopardise all that.

It took him a long time to agree to appear. Like any addict, part of his recovery programme was not being rushed into making quick decisions. He'd already turned down an invitation to the first World Seniors tournament because he didn't feel ready to face being away from his treatment plan.

It was a big deal for him, travelling overseas for the first time again, and facing the demons that playing snooker, and especially playing snooker back in Sheffield, could bring. Then of course there was Jimmy, his lifelong friend but someone he had been in the very darkest of places with. At points in their playing careers Kirk and Jimmy were cocaine addicts. And what was worse was they were earning enough money to fund the addiction. For Jimmy it was more of a phase – a blow-out that started after losing to Davis in the 1984 World Final. Sadly for Kirk it became a way of life, and one that offered him an escape from his loneliness.

Both had film-star lifestyles and while commercially for snooker they were great, this wasn't a film script. They were living it for real. Snooker was at its peak: during that 1984 match Hollywood superstar Donald Sutherland visited Wembley. He arrived just at the start of the frame where Kirk made the 147, he left straight after the final black. He later commented that he'd only ever seen one frame of snooker and Kirk Stevens in a white suit had shot the 'perfect' game. He'd seen everything he needed in the space of 15 minutes!

Amazingly, Kirk Stevens never failed a drugs test and was never disciplined in any way by the WPBSA for substance abuse. It was only after a claim by fellow player Silvino Francisco that Kirk himself owned up to his drugs problems. Francisco accused him of taking stimulants during the final of the 1985 Dulux British Open; Francisco was subsequently fined by the World Snooker Association for the comments. He had already won the match and the title, so his motive for accusing Kirk was puzzling.

In 1997, Silvino Francisco was arrested for smuggling cannabis, and served three years in prison; out of the two it's the South African who has the drugs conviction, not Kirk. Some may say that's karma. Others could say that without the accusation being made, and subsequent admission from Kirk, he might never have got help.

Cliff Thorburn always said a 'clean' Kirk Stevens was a good enough player to win the World Championship. Sadly, being clean at that time was a far bigger challenge than surviving 17 days in Sheffield. He struggled on and off the table until the 1993 season but then retired from the tour to go home for treatment. Far from not playing though, Kirk won the Canadian Open Championship in 1997, 1998, 2000, 2002 and 2008 – so I knew if we got him to a Legends he would still be able to hold a cue.

I can't overemphasise the part Cliff played in getting Kirk to agree to the shows and travel to the UK. He was with me when we met Kirk at Heathrow, and although they were both on edge, we travelled up to Sheffield together and having Cliff in the car helped calm and reassure Kirk.

Their friendship spanned 40 years. Kirk had first played Cliff when he was just 12 years old. In those days, in Toronto, you could play Cliff for whatever money you wanted. Kirk took two dollars from his hockey bag and took on the man who, in his words, was 'even then one of the best players in the world'. Cliff recalls playing him and trying not to take the money; Kirk insisted he took it. Cliff says it's probably the dirtiest money he's ever made!

We arranged a practice session at the Star Academy in Sheffield.

China's number-one player Ding Junhui was there when we arrived. His English is not great and I don't think he had any idea who Kirk was when he shook his hand.

Kirk wanted to see Jimmy; it had been ten years at least. I didn't think Jimmy was arriving until the morning of the show – wrong again! Jimmy was already in Sheffield, on his own schedule as usual.

It was a weird build-up. Kirk was on edge about seeing Jimmy again, and Jimmy was worried about seeing Kirk. Goodness knows how close these two had taken each other to death through their use of hard drugs; I guess it bonds you infinitely.

Fate stepped in and solved the anxiety for both men...

As we were checking into the hotel Jimmy emerged from the lift, so they basically bumped into each other. They hugged and both cried; I joked later that it was like a scene from *Brokeback Mountain*. I think for those 10 seconds the last 30 years flashed through their minds: here were two 50-year-old men almost celebrating the fact that, despite every attempt to kill themselves and each other with drink and drugs, they had somehow survived. It felt like the reunion deserved to be somewhere better than a hotel reception.

Jimmy still lived in a world where he could have a drink. That was a place Kirk could not go, and Jimmy had already suggested to everyone on the team that we shouldn't drink around him.

Just as I'd put Higgins back in a green shirt, I was determined to get Kirk back in the white suit he was famous for. There was no way he was going to allow me to put him in white trousers, but he did concede that the white waistcoat would be a nice touch; he also wore a lounge tie, again very 'afternoon session 1980s'. The 2013 Champion of Champions Invitational Event brought back the wearing of lounge ties; I think it worked, and I have ties for afternoon sessions in the World Seniors Tour events. It feels traditional.

The BBC was all over the fact that Kirk was back at the

Crucible for Legends; it made for a perfect feature for the 2011 Championship. We recorded the piece in the hotel in the afternoon of the event and Kirk really opened up. It was quite emotional.

Talking about his addiction he claimed: 'I'm grateful for every day that I'm sober; this is just another gift of sobriety for me. I'm back here playing snooker at the Crucible. I'm free, I feel that I'm free today, finally.'

Coming back to the Crucible was something he thought would never happen. Looking back, he claims doing it was part of an important step of his recovery. For many years snooker was associated with drinking, drugs and despair. In Kirk's world they were grouped together and you could not have one without the other. He had slowly broken that chain, and here he was back at the home of snooker playing snooker without needing the other vices. He was indeed 'free'.

Kirk was going to play Jimmy that night. He got a great reception and actually took the opening frame from the Whirlwind.

I'm not sure how much serious snooker was going on, but Michaela had chalked off officiating another legend, and another important step in the recovery of Kirk Stevens, Sober Snooker Player, had taken place.

We still keep in touch and I'd like to think Snooker Legends played a small part in his recovery and connected him again with the sport that made and broke him.

At the point of writing this book Kirk remains 'free' but every day remains a battle. I wish him well.

CHAPTER 12

PC DAVID RATHBAND

Kirk Stevens wasn't the only special guest that night in Sheffield. In 2010, Northumbria Police Force were deployed to apprehend Raoul Moat, a 37-year-old man from Newcastle upon Tyne who was on the run after shooting three people in two days. His victims were ex-girlfriend Samantha Stobbart, her new partner Chris Brown, and PC David Rathband.

David remained in hospital for nearly three weeks and was permanently blinded from gunshot wounds fired into his police car. Moat remained on the run for days; the manhunt was national news, as was the recovery of his only surviving victim – a policeman who just happened to be in the wrong place at the wrong time doing his job trying to protect us.

In February 2011 I took a call from Northumbria Police. David was a snooker fan and wanted to know about attending our event at the Crucible.

I didn't want to ask the obvious question about not being able to see, but the guy who called, a fellow police officer called

Serge, explained David would enjoy the atmosphere of the venue and also he himself would communicate the action in his colleague's ear.

I had no hesitation in arranging complimentary tickets for David and Serge; he was a hero in my eyes. I spoke with David himself before the event: he called to thank me for arranging the tickets and to get details of the hotel we were staying at. He had a good knowledge of snooker and had enjoyed playing before the accident. He had always wanted to visit the Crucible.

During 2011 we had started introducing an auction of memorabilia at the events. I was never entirely comfortable with the concept, but we bought the items initially from a shop that Jimmy had a share in and all the players would get their food and drink covered from the money we made on the take. The more we made, the better the pizza we had afterwards – that's how it worked.

On the Crucible night Jimmy suggested we took it a stage further and raffled off a frame to play against him. It all felt a bit 'market stall' to me but he convinced me we could get someone to part with a grand, and we were on 50/50 of course! Typical Jimmy.

A few celebrities were in the audience that night. I'd just started doing the short-lived *Bullseye* darts tour and former world champions John Lowe and Bob Anderson had come along, as had former snooker player Tony Knowles and Nottingham Forest football legend John McGovern.

The bidding got to about £300 and stalled. It was a flop really, nowhere near the £1,000 we thought we'd get. JV was doing his best to drive it, to build it up as a one-off chance to play in the Crucible against the Whirlwind. Another celebrity from the quiz show *Eggheads*, CJ De Mooi, jumped in with £350; CJ is a keen snooker player and is seen at a few tournaments.

From the back of the Crucible by the curtains, my eyesight wasn't good enough to see exactly who was left bidding, but it was John Parrott who told me that David Rathband had started bidding. This was uncomfortable.

People stopped bidding and David won the chance to play Jimmy for £500. I had that sick feeling, and any colour Jimmy had in his face drained too. If we weren't careful this could turn into a very poor joke. I'd just charged a blind national hero £500 to play a frame of snooker in the Crucible.

David was helped into the arena; you could just feel that everyone was on edge. JV took control and David broke the ice himself by cracking a gag about playing a 'blinding shot'. Everyone relaxed and laughed with him, no one relaxing more than me.

JV lined him up for every shot, he made a few balls and the audience went wild. There is no doubt that John Virgo saved my arse that night.

We never auctioned a frame again and the whole auction of memorabilia at events soon disappeared as well. And of course we never took the £500 from David, despite him offering it twice.

After the event I spent about ten minutes talking with David, and we shared the breakfast table the next morning. He was so upbeat and positive and interested in what I was doing, and how the tour was going. I was fascinated by the way he was able to navigate his way round a full English breakfast despite not being able to see what he was eating.

He particularly liked Michaela; she made a fuss of him. He also insisted on buying us a drink. As one final gesture Jimmy gave him the Snooker Legends trophy to keep as a memory of his night playing him – he was one very unique man who I thought would go on to be a real inspiration for others.

On 29th February 2012, only ten months after this night, saddled with depression, David sadly took his own life. It affected us all.

It was my privilege to meet him. Rest in peace, PC Rathband. I hope you're enjoying a game or two up there in heaven.

PROCURING A NUGGET

There was one glaring omission from the list of legends I'd used so far: 'The Nugget' Steve Davis.

I'd never approached Steve because he was Barry's man, and at the time I didn't think the success of the tour was being well received within Matchroom Sport. For some reason I never thought he'd agree to play at Legends as it would be seen as being disloyal to Barry. I needn't have worried. He said yes to appearing at a night in Stoke against Dennis immediately.

I billed it as a '1985 World Snooker Final rematch' with Dennis playing Steve, John Virgo doing the commentary. It was Saturday 14th May, the day of the 2011 FA Cup Final, which normally wouldn't have been a problem. But when I'd agreed this date six months earlier, who would have bet on Stoke City reaching the Cup Final? They'd never made the final before, and they'd last reached a semi-final back in 1972! Typical, bloody typical.

The town was deserted; all the sports fans had made a pilgrimage down the M1 to Wembley to see Stoke play Manchester City.

Eighty-eight thousand packed the new stadium; less than four hundred came to watch us.

Sometimes as a promoter you deserve to get caught out. I wouldn't have dreamed of putting on a show in Manchester, Liverpool or near Chelsea on Cup Final Day, but Stoke? Come on, you have to agree that was bad luck!

The night itself went well. Steve was new to Legends but a master of working a crowd at exhibitions, and of course with Dennis they already had a 'script' they had perfected over many of these types of shows.

If anything, I had too many entertainers on the bill. With Steve, Dennis and JV telling jokes, the snooker sometimes got lost, but it still went down to the final black of course.

I never, ever stage a Legends' result. It's important that the public know they are seeing players going out there wanting to win as badly as if they were playing for the world title. I didn't fix this result but Steve and Dennis found it difficult to break away from what they usually do. No one complained and I can't even remember who potted the final black. It was probably Dennis; history dictates it usually is!

That was the only show Steve did in 2011, but by 2012 he had become a permanent fixture on the tour, and of course in 2013 he had his own little stint in the Australian outback which brought him to a new audience, much like it had with Jimmy.

Steve retired in 2016 and received a great send-off at the Crucible. He remains on our screens with the BBC as a pundit, but aside from the odd exhibition he has very little to do with the sport now. He's found a new lease of life as DJ Thundermuscle, swapping the baize for a DJ kit. It's now places like Glastonbury and Knifeworld he performs at rather than the Crucible.

Steve made it clear when I got the World Seniors that he wouldn't play in it; he had no desire to play competitively again or spend time practising. He'd still do some exhibitions and was vocal publicly about how he felt I was the right man to take over the tour. At the Irish Masters in 2018 he covered for Stephen Hendry and played Dennis Taylor one last time in front of a packed house in Goffs. He arrived having had no practice but with a huge smile on his face, happy to help out and say one final goodbye to the Irish fans who had seen him victorious in that arena a staggering eight times... he beat Taylor, he beat Parrott and then he beat Jonathan Bagley; he won the whole event and only dropped a frame!

As long as he is willing and able to hold a cue I'll always use him... After all, it's never bad to have a six-time world champion and one-time Senior Irish Masters champion on the bill is it? Class is permanent.

CHAPTER 14

MEETING RONNIE

Many of the legends I've worked with have superstitions, and as you can see by the numbering of this and the previous two chapters, I'm afflicted by one as well. Some players are terrified of changing their pre-match routines: they always put a certain match shoe on first, or they save a lucky shirt for finals, etc. For me, I grew up fascinated by space, or more importantly, the Apollo *space programme that took Neil Armstrong to the Moon in 1969. Apollo 13 was slated to be the third moon landing, but a defective oxygen tank meant it became more about a race to get home and save the lives of astronauts Lovell, Haise and Swigert. After that tragedy no other spacecraft, or NASA mission, has ever carried the number 13. From the age of seven, when I first read about this, I decided to follow suit.*

When I started the Legends Tour it was not for people like Ronnie O'Sullivan, but when the game's only global superstar wants to join the team and play in some shows, then it would have been commercial suicide to turn him down.

I have always been respectful to the older legends like Cliff Thorburn and Dennis Taylor, so you will never see a show staged with Ronnie playing just them one on one. It wouldn't work on any level and I wouldn't want to put either of those former world champions through it.

Ronnie used to dislike exhibitions: fact. Before we came along, the term 'exhibition' to him meant grotty clubs, drunken people, and the pressure of making a maximum 147 break every frame, on substandard tables with crap balls. It was a no-win situation in his eyes and he admires how Jimmy is able to do it night after night. It's fair to say I changed his opinion on this during our 2016 tour.

At Legends we try to recreate, as best we possibly can, tournament conditions. I am anal about the organisation: everything has to run like clockwork and we must finish a show feeling we've done everything within our power to provide the best value for money we can.

Of course I can't pot the balls for them, but with at least two legends playing each night, and sometimes eight playing at a Legends Cup, they are not all going to forget where the pockets are.

We are also able to protect Ronnie. Sure, he has to make himself accessible to the people who pay for their VIP experience, but there is a line people can't cross. He doesn't always find the hospitality side of it easy, but he understands he has to do it. His work and training with Eurosport has helped massively and given him a different perspective on the value of embracing this work.

I've been a close friend of Ronnie for about seven years now. Within Ronnie's snooker world you could argue that I'm due a testimonial or a gold carriage clock for long service! I've seen four or five managers come and go, close friends become strangers overnight.

There is a side of Ronnie that most people never see; he is unbelievably generous, very funny and good company. He is also well read and shows a real passion when he speaks on a subject that really interests him, cookery and running being the two obvious examples. Ask him about Mo Farah's split times over 5,000 metres, or his resting heart rate now compared to 2010 after a track session, and he won't be found wanting. He's also pretty good if you want to know where to enjoy the best food in East London – and he can usually get you a table sorted too!

Ronnie is also incredibly sensitive. I know he was upset at the way his book *Running* was serialised. Even though he had no control on how they edited it, he was on the phone explaining to those who were cast in a light that was completely out of context how sorry he was.

The boring truth is, in five years I've seen him drunk twice – well drunk, I might add – and we've been out socially only a handful of times.

Outside of tournaments, and away from his 'work', he is a family man who dotes on his kids, does his running, likes to cook, and sits on the sofa drinking tea. I've seen Liam Gallagher text him to come for a drink, and David Beckham has asked for his number on more than one occasion. It simply doesn't interest him.

It doesn't make for rock and roll but that's the lifestyle that appeals to him. Maybe he did create hell before I met him, but I have always thought the problem is the real Ronnie O'Sullivan is actually quite a boring fella who just happens to be the best in the world at what he does.

We hit it off from day one, mainly, I think, because I've never tried to change him or impose anything on him. I've never pressurised him into doing a show for me even when commercially there were times I really needed him for ticket sales, and he knows it doesn't matter to me if he never plays a Legends show again.

Don't get me wrong. I have done a lot for him, both personally and commercially, but it's a two-way street.

Ronnie doesn't have a coach any more, save Steve Peters. He is a player who performs on instinct although he remains a student of the game. If he feels something isn't right he will spend time watching old videos from 2012 of himself playing when he feels he played his best snooker. He isn't watching the trophy presentations, or the plaudits from Messrs Davis, Hendry and Parrott: he is studying how he was standing, the rhythm of his backswing, the bridge position, in fact anything he can associate as a small trigger to attend to a current perceived glitch. He has a natural ability with both hands but he has certainly worked at it too. He is like a swan, serene to the eye but paddling hard beneath the water.

Within his current trusted circle I am probably the most knowledgeable about the 'game' and we do talk about the technical aspects of snooker, especially when I am picking balls for him at tournaments. I can also sense when to talk and when to give space, and I know never to patronise him. If he is hitting the ball bad and asks if I think he is, I won't go the other way and say it's great, it's in your head, don't worry. I'm more likely to say, let's do a few more hours or let's bin it and get a Chinese. Come back tomorrow.

He may be the best player in the world but he suffers the same self-doubt and anxiety as everyone else.

At work, he can be grumpy, impatient and rude, but as I say to him, when you've been stuck in the same job for 28 years; you're bound to have a bad day once in a while, aren't you?

And of course everything he does is magnified because of his commercial value to the sport. Everything Ronnie O'Sullivan does in snooker makes the papers. Without him the sport's commercial value to sponsors would suffer, as he proved when he took his last sabbatical in 2012.

But he is a free spirit, very much like Alex Higgins was in his day. He refuses to toe the line all the time and I'm sure if you ask Barry Hearn, honestly he would probably agree that even though Ronnie can drive him mad, it's not a bad thing for the sport.

There are few characters left nowadays – he is to snooker what Tiger Woods is to golf, what Phil Taylor is to darts, and what David Beckham was to football. However, when Tiger dropped away there was Rory McIlroy and Jordan Spieth, when Phil started losing there was Van Gerwen, and when Beckham retired, two blokes called Ronaldo and Messi filled the void. Seriously, within snooker who is going to fill the gap left by Ronnie O'Sullivan when he stops playing?

Sure, there are other good players, but you can't turn a Selby or a Murphy into a Ronnie. It's not in their nature and why should they change? Even Mark Selby would admit that though he may be a multiple world champion, untouchable World Number 1, and wins many big tournaments, the sport is still primarily, at least from the media angle, all about Ronnie.

Will he turn up? How will he play? 'Look, he lost', 'Look, he's cut his hair', 'Now he's talking like a bloody robot', 'What the hell are those trainers about?' 'Give him his trophy'– everything he does seems to be newsworthy but largely rubbish.

Ronnie never chose to be famous; he just wanted to play snooker. It wasn't his fault that the job and career he chose came with all the other 'stuff' – stuff he is not that comfortable with even after doing it for more than 25 years.

I first met Ronnie in 2010. We'd just finished our first Legends Tour and Jimmy was playing him in Colchester to raise money for Ronnie's PA who had breast cancer. Jimmy knew if he could get Ronnie involved, then not only would Legends have someone who could sell tickets like Alex Higgins, but the Whirlwind himself would be in for lots more work himself.

He was with a guy called Robbie who had shared a prison

floor with Ronnie's father and had been tasked with helping Ronnie out.

I got on with Robbie straight away. He was very calmly spoken but what the fuck he knew about snooker I will never know! He'd make a cracking Barry Gibb lookalike though.

That night Ronnie was quite quiet, subdued. The event certainly wasn't organised like a Legends night, and I think he would have quite happily written a cheque for double the amount the night was going to raise to not be there at all. Jimmy gave a night for free to play him; I think he played a few shows in prison for Ronnie as well. Ronnie would repay the favour by playing at Jimmy's testimonial. They'd give each other the shirt off their backs.

It's a very special friendship. First there was Alex, then Jimmy picked up the mantle. Ronnie carried on from Jimmy… After Ronnie it feels like we have a dodo situation looming. As Stephen Hendry said during the 2014 World, after Ronnie destroyed Shaun Murphy, 'Will someone please step up?' – poignant words that refer to snooker as a whole now in 2018.

I was in the dressing room in Colchester but I felt like a bit of an intruder, the exact kind of hanger-on I despise at my own events. I really had no purpose and kept quite quiet. Ronnie himself asked me if I did the Legend shows full-time. As I explained, at the time my company actually did mostly children's theatre, including the national tour of *Thomas the Tank Engine*.

A spark, eye contact… 'Little Ronnie loves that,' he said. 'Can you get me some tickets?'

Bugger that, I thought, I'll bring him to you and we can travel the Trans-Siberian if you want!

I exchanged numbers with the Bee Gee and we set up some tickets for him to come to one of my shows at the Orchard Theatre in Dartford. Ronnie came with his mum, Maria, and his two children, Ronnie Junior and Lily.

It was a show I was pretty proud of. We'd used the trains from

First Meeting
Me pictured with my team and Jimmy the first night I met him and proposed a Legends Tour.

Clever Boy
Alex back at the Crucible Theatre for Snooker Legends. The day before he had discharged himself from hospital, and still wears the identity bracelet on his right wrist with cuffs rolled up for all to see.

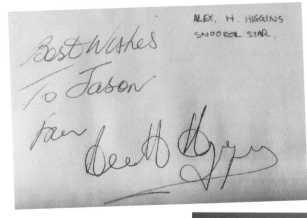

Left: The Autograph I got in 1981 from Alex. I wasn't there, in bed with ear ache.

Right: The 1988 Cornish U21 Snooker Champion.

Left: Cornwall, my real home.

I produced and created two theatre shows in 2010, Snooker Legends with
Jimmy and Alex and Bullseye with Bristow, Lowe and Anderson.

Above left: 8th April 2010 Alex walks back into the crucible theatre for one final match.

Above right: John Virgo, my co-pilot on this crazy journey.

Below: I was Jimmy's guest as he won the 2010 World Seniors Title, little did I know 8 years later I would be running that tour.

Above left: I have a massive amount of respect for Barry Hearn, he made it really tough for me at times but also always kept his word when he said he would help.

Middle left: PC David Rathband playing at The Crucible.

Above right: The Greatest Ladies Snooker player ever, Reanne Evans. I've looked after here since 2014 and she's a top girl.

Below: Taking Kirk Stevens back to the Crucible in 2011 was really emotional for everyone on the team.

Above: Finally snared Dracula, Ray Reardon picked up his cue again as our special guest in Plymouth.

Below: After 17 shows in Year One, the legends presented me with a memento at our final show in Doncaster.

Right: Snooker Royalty. I couldn't believe these three legends were working with me at my Legends Cup Event in Bedworth.

Left: Life Before Snooker... one of my shows and the one that got me introduced to Ronnie. Ronnie Junior loved Thomas.

Below: Michaela Tabb, been there since Day 1, seen the struggle and enjoyed the triumphs.

Above: On tour in Cornwall and had to educate him with some proper food!

Above: The job has had its perks for sure… here with Steven Gerrard, Frank Bruno and Pelé.

Below: Dinner with friends in Romania.

the worldwide tour and I'd reworked and rewritten the script for the UK stage. I'd also directed the performance.

To give you an idea, the Thomas train itself cost nearly $1 million to build, and it was only on loan; I didn't own it. I say this because we had to be very protective of it. Not only did it weigh over a ton and was capable of eight miles per hour, but if it pushed you up against a wall it could kill you. The health and safety procedures around the operating of the train were extensive. Only our stage manager and the actor who drove the train in the show were allowed anywhere near it.

And then, of course, there was the latex face.

The latex face on Thomas cost about $100,000. It was fully animatronic and felt like real skin – not that you *ever* touched it, mind you. It was so fragile that the moment Thomas was off-stage, or between shows, a protective cover would go over it. If we damaged it in any way, or split the latex, you could not repair it. As well as the cover, signs always adorned the prop clearly stating, 'Under no circumstances must you touch the face'. If we had to do photocalls, or even maintenance, we had another member of the stage-management team on hand to make sure that you never touched the face. Don't touch the face, don't touch the face…

Photocall with Ronnie and his kids and what does his daughter do? Practically tries hanging herself off the face, pulling his mouth, pushing his eyes about.

It was one of those really awkward moments where panic spread around everyone on stage. Luckily no harm was done, but as a mickey-take the next time I visited a performance of the show, the sign had been changed. It still said: 'Under no circumstances touch the face' and underneath in Sharpie had been added: 'unless your dad plays snooker'.

It was very funny.

After the performance, Ronnie said to me that we should do a few Legends shows. Just two months later we did our first show in Blackburn and streamed it on the internet.

The date fitted perfectly as both Jimmy and Ronnie had been in Blackpool for the Sky Shoot-out the day before. They were both sharp, and boy did it show. Of the eight frames they played they made six centuries. It was ridiculous. The good news is we had it on film – I've sold a fair few DVDs of that night, I can tell you. Suddenly the snooker had been raised to a whole new level; these two played some of the best stuff I've ever seen.

Ronnie was now part of Snooker Legends. As we did more shows, our friendship grew and I started helping him out at a few tournaments. We took snooker back to the Barbican in York, the year before World Snooker relocated the UK there, and Damien Hirst came along.

It was a buzz having one of the world's richest artists there and the picture he did for me – I say picture, it was more of a squiggle of a shark, but who cares! – is framed on my wall. He is a really cool guy, so good for calming Ronnie and breaking the tension, especially in Sheffield.

Damien is also a snooker nut, and incredibly generous, but he really doesn't give a fuck, about anything. It's quite refreshing to see someone who has elevated themselves to a position where they basically make up the rules. Some of the art he has done for Ronnie is priceless, and I know he did a very special piece for Stephen Hendry too.

I was around at the time he won the 2012 World's but I didn't go to the final. It was shortly after this that the story broke that Ronnie was going to take a break from snooker and was refusing to sign the player's contract.

Commercially this was very bad for snooker: the world champion and the game's most prized possession was putting his feet up because he had been advised that the player's contract was too restrictive. It was a mess, and the truth is it could easily have been sorted if Django (his manager at the time) and Barry Hearn had sat round a table with Ronnie and explained what each clause of the contract meant.

Then again, if Ronnie had carried on playing that season I would never have been part of the 2013 World's comeback story. The Rocket would make snooker history and I got to be co-pilot.

CHAPTER 15

TED LOWE – THE GODFATHER

'For those of you who are watching in black and white, the pink is next to the green.'

There is a common recurring argument that generally pops up whenever a tournament is televised on any channel other than BBC: 'Who's been the best commentator?'

In some people's eyes you need to have played the game at the highest level to have the authority to commentate on it – hence why when Hendry, Davis or Parrott talk, it's tough to challenge it because they have been there and done it.

But playing at the highest level didn't make Jimmy White a great commentator; in fact he was pretty average before he joined what I call the cast of 'Men Behaving Badly' on the Eurosport couch with Ron and Neal Foulds.

There is one widely regarded 'Daddy' of snooker commentary who set the standards by which everyone is now measured.

For anyone who grew up watching snooker on TV, Ted Lowe was a constant companion, his voice associated with so many great moments from the sport. His commentary started in the days of black-and-white TV; this is where the famous quote at the top of this chapter comes from.

Ted wasn't a player; he was the manager of the Leicester Square Hall, at the time the home of billiards and snooker. He was a close associate of the all-time-great Joe Davis, the 15-time world champion.

One day, BBC's regular commentator Raymond Glendenning had lost his voice; Ted stepped in to cover Raymond, and he found himself remaining at the microphone for 50 years! Ted would commentate from the audience and so had to keep the level of his voice as low as possible so as not to disturb the players. Hence the 'whispering' style and subsequent nickname, 'Whispering Ted'.

In the 1960s the controller of BBC2 was wildlife expert David Attenborough. He wanted something to show off the new colour TV service, and with its coloured balls and cheap production costs, snooker was ideal. Ted came up with the idea for the series *Pot Black*.

After Ray Reardon joined our tour, and Kirk Stevens played in the Crucible, I spoke to JV about getting Ted along to be a special guest when the 2011 tour went to Brighton, as that was where he lived.

JV thought it was a marvellous idea, as without Ted, JV himself would never have never got a break behind the microphone. Jimmy was also especially close to Ted and they enjoyed a bottle of Dom Pérignon on more than one occasion after tournaments.

Ted loved the idea, but did explain he was 90 years old now, so JV would have to help him if he got tired! He was also worried about how he was going to get home that late at night after the show. I believe his wife Jean was a bit younger but certainly way beyond driving age.

Jimmy stepped in and booked a limousine, with champagne of course, to bring Ted, Jean, her brother and his wife to the theatre.

They even discussed leaving early so they could take the longer route along the coast.

'Best get two bottles,' Jimmy remarked.

We were all lifted by Ted agreeing to come and join the team. Since Alex's death, the Legends' mood had been a little sombre.

Ted was renowned, and loved, for making the odd gaffe on-air. As well as the black-and-white TV quote, he was once commentating on the great Fred Davis at the World Championship. Fred was 64 at the time and struggling to get one leg on the edge of the table in order to reach a long shot. He gave up and switched to play the shot with his other hand.

Ted uttered the immortal words live on the BBC: 'Well, Fred Davis is 64 now, he is getting on a bit and is having trouble getting his leg over.' Not content with that he followed it up by saying, 'He prefers to use his left hand instead.'

Dennis tells the story at every exhibition and even after hearing it 50 times it still makes me laugh.

About a month before the show was due to play, Ted called, the whispering voice like smooth treacle down the phone. He explained he'd been suffering from a bit of a cold and was worried he might not be able to make it unless he could shake it off. He wanted to record a message to play to the audience just in case. To be honest I wasn't overly worried but he said he'd record it anyway.

A few days later a letter arrived with an accompanying TDK C60 cassette tape! I guess Ted didn't have an iPhone.

The letter was beautifully handwritten by Ted himself but I had no machine any more that even played a cassette, so I placed it in the drawer.

He phoned the next day to make sure I had received it and apologised for the singing! Singing? Now the contents of the tape intrigued me.

Ted was feeling a bit better but he was worried about all the autographs he would have to sign as he had arthritis in his hands.

We therefore sent the pictures down in advance so he could sign them at his leisure.

At the Crucible for the early rounds the table is separated by a dividing 'curtain'. They call it the curtain but in reality it's a solid piece of scenery that is hoisted in and out before play and probably weighs half a ton. The photo I chose from the David Muscroft Collection, the only Crucible photographer at the time, for him to sign was the famous shot when, live on TV, as Ted was closing off the broadcast, the curtain started coming in. Ted was right underneath it. Instead of moving to avoid a collision, which could have put the camera out of focus, he simply bent his knees to avoid being hit on the head whilst still continuing to speak. What a professional! The moment was captured beautifully and Ted loved the idea of having that as his official photo.

Generally, modern-day players have a threshold on the amount of autographs they will sign before they walk off; it's probably boredom as much as anything. I don't think Jimmy has gone more than a day or so in the last 35 years without signing at least one photo, train ticket, body part or piece of underwear!

Also, by the time they get to the tenth or so request the signature itself starts resembling just a scribble. I've learned the hard way in Legends not to try to get players to sign too many things in one go as the ones at the end become pretty illegible. Then, of course, the moment you ask them to add anything more than just their name, like a dedication or 'best wishes', it becomes a real issue for some!

I understand before an important match, or during their meals or practice, then they shouldn't be expected to stop to sign photos and autographs. But I think as long as it's managed correctly, a polite fan should never be turned down from getting their hero's signature.

Of course the invention of the 'selfie' has made it even worse. Ronnie, for example, doesn't mind doing the pictures, but what drives him mad is people not knowing how to use their phones.

What was supposed to be a quick arm round him for a snap turns into a survival technique of sharing body warmth with a stranger whilst someone struggles with the phone.

Ted Lowe signed every photo meticulously, and added the phrase 'memories of pleasure'. They became real collectors' items and mine is one of the few pieces of snooker memorabilia I have that I really treasure.

The photos got returned to me, I called Ted to thank him and we talked about the pick-up time for the limousine. The show itself was only a few weeks away. I thought everything was fine.

Ted passed away on 1st May, and never got to commentate at the Snooker Legends show in Brighton.

Jimmy made sure his widow Jean got the limo ride, with champagne, and shed a tear like all of us when his voice from beyond the grave was played to the crowd in the Brighton Centre that night. It all felt like Ted had a premonition to record the message. JV was particularly emotional.

The 2011 tour continued on, and we went north of the border and visited Scotland for the first time. I'd booked a punishing schedule for my team, four venues in four days. London to Penrith, Penrith to Glasgow, Glasgow to Inverness, Inverness to Aberdeen!

JP saw an opportunity to fill the days playing some of Scotland's finest golf courses. He still says those few days with Dennis and Cliff, playing links golf in the day and snooker in the evenings, were his favourite times.

Dennis always partnered JP, and Cliff would play with the local member who had got them on the course. It was usually only for a tenner, but if Dennis and JP won, Cliff would hand it over graciously and the world would know the outcome, Dennis made sure of that.

If Cliff won – sometimes it happened! – then two scruffy fivers or a few coins would be pulled from Dennis' golf bag and passed over via a secret handshake in the car park. It was pretty competitive.

The tour ended in Grimsby on the 13th July. We played 31 dates in 2011 and the boys had made 35 centuries, including Jimmy's second 147 maximum break. It was a great year, but we'd lost Ted, and John Parrott had also lost his manager, Phil Miller.

Phil was the man who discovered John at 13 and stayed with him throughout his whole playing career. He was a real help to me in the early days. He attended a few shows and always tried to support what we were doing. Snooker lost another good man the day Phil Miller passed; JP lost a father figure.

CHAPTER 16

THE CHAMPIONS LEAGUE
FINAL 2011

Midway through the 2011 tour I booked a couple of Irish venues: Belfast in Northern Ireland for our Alex Higgins tribute night and Goffs in Kildare, home for many years to the Benson & Hedges Irish Masters.

Annoyingly there was a dead day between the two shows. That meant extra hotel costs for our touring party, which actually had six players on it, as Kirk had flown in again from Toronto and Ken Doherty had joined us. I got an approach from Dundalk FC about staging an event, and after checking out the map, I saw it lay perfectly between the two current Irish dates.

I usually work with theatres that have their own marketing departments and databases; this goes a long way towards selling tickets. Although Dundalk was a football club, I still assumed they would have a fan base of season-ticket holders, and we were only looking to shift 500 tickets to cover our costs.

They could fit the date in. Happy days... But then two things happened: Dundalk FC sold tickets about as well as they kept clean sheets, and Manchester United beat Schalke of Germany

6-1 in the semi-final of the Champions League and would face Barcelona FC on the night we were due to play this extra show. It was the Stoke FA Cup scenario all over again.

I managed to work with a local marketing lady who got us a complimentary hotel, which saved some money, and as I was on a fee to cover costs, I wasn't really worried.

JV and Ken were gutted. Both big Manchester United fans, they didn't want to work on the night their team played in a cup final, especially against the world's most glamorous opponents who had beaten them previously in the 2009 final.

Of course Dundalk FC now had the perfect excuse as to why tickets weren't selling: the football match. When I tried explaining that to sell tickets, people first need to know the event is on, it fell on deaf ears.

The solution was simple, but one which my event team weren't going to like: we'd play the exhibition in the afternoon and have a Champions League party at the hotel in the evening! It meant my event team finishing at midnight in Belfast and setting up at 7am in Dundalk; you can probably guess how popular I was! The €50 bribes were in force that night.

However, what seemed like a 'fill-in' date, with no expectations and nothing but aggravation in its planning, actually turned into an historic show.

We get quite a few celebrities visiting our shows, usually because of their friendships with Jimmy. In Dundalk it was no different and we welcomed one guest who was certainly larger than life. Glenn Ross, known by his nickname 'Big Daddy', was a former Irish strongman and powerlifter, having been Britain's Strongest Man on five occasions. He was also a snooker fan.

We soon found out that strong men don't shake hands; they hug! I seriously thought he'd put my back out, and Jimmy felt winded – this bloke was enormous. When he asked Jimmy for his chalk as a memento at the end of the show the Whirlwind was happy to oblige; he didn't hang round for a second hug though –

I'm not sure his spine would have taken it. A perfect gentleman and very quietly spoken, Glenn could probably have carried the snooker table out on his back.

In Dundalk it was Jimmy's turn to be the person the raffle winner would get to play – as usual he was thrilled!

We'd ended up with 300 in. I was going to lose a bit of money, as the football club now couldn't guarantee the fee they'd agreed in the contract, but it wasn't a catastrophe. There hadn't been anything spectacular about the snooker in the first half; it was quite cold in the room and the table was running slow. It felt weird doing a show in the afternoon and everyone seemed a bit uninterested and lethargic.

The raffle winner was pulled out and down came this middle-aged man, delighted to have got the chance to challenge the great Jimmy White. Jimmy duly presented the cue to him, at which point he told JV that he had his own cue and the Mrs had just gone to the car to get it. It was quite a funny moment and JV milked it.

Another little thing we do is put the winner's name up on the scoreboard so it looks all official. As usual JV enquired as to his name. 'It's Terry,' he said. 'What's your surname, bud?' said JV, knowing that there are two lines of text on the software for the scoreboard so you can display the player's full name.

'I want to be known as Tornado Terry,' he said, bold as brass. The room laughed. Was this guy having a laugh or was he being serious?

As we were still filling time for his 'wand' to arrive from the boot of some charabanc in the car park, JV tried to see just how serious he was.

'So, Tornado Terry, you know that's Tony Drago's nickname, don't you?'

'I'm quicker than him,' quipped Terry.

'Shame your wife's not been a bit quicker getting your cue, Terry,' said JV.

It was obvious the guy thought he could play a bit, and when the cue duly arrived the mandatory handshake took place and Terry won the toss.

'I'll let you break,' said Tornado with a small touch of bravado in his voice. By now he must have put half a block of chalk on his tip. The professional player usually lets the amateur break off, bit of etiquette. Jimmy wasn't too pleased about being summoned to the table to break off. He smashed the cue ball at about a hundred miles an hour into the back of the pack from the top cushion.

These frames aren't about the pros proving they can play. They are about someone playing their hero on a match table and winning a cue – unless of course you brought you own cue with you!

The balls split all over the table and Terry approached the table. There was purpose in his stride and he meant business. He hadn't got past the baulk line when a rogue red ricocheted off about 12 other balls and dropped in the middle pocket. The crowd fell about.

'Sit down, Tornado,' said JV.

At that point Terry had no idea he'd be sitting down for a while, but at least he'd have the best seat in the house as a bit of snooker history was about to be made.

Jimmy potted seven reds and seven blacks and we had all started to get that maximum 147-break feeling.

Although all the reds were spread around the table it actually was a disadvantage to Jimmy, as he had to navigate after each red ball back to the black through a maze of other balls. Also one huge disadvantage of playing the break-off shot like he did is that you cannot fail to send the pink ball up the table.

The pink in this frame was actually sat almost frozen to the baulk cushion. It made a clearance seem unlikely but we could all dream.

Remember, to this point Terry hadn't even had a shot; we were on the verge of the first-ever 147 being made from the break-off shot... but we had that pesky *bándearg* (pink) to overcome first.

Ten reds, then eleven... Before long we'd got to the yellow and the place was buzzing. Fortunately a member of the crowd had been recording the frame, so history was at least being documented, albeit via a Handycam shaking like an earthquake had struck County Louth. I would have said Tornado would have been more apt than Earthquake but Terry was sat quiet in his seat. You had the feeling that trip to the car to get his cue was going to be a waste of Mrs Tornado's shoe leather!

By the time we got to the blue ball every shot was being met with a huge cheer. JV was trying to calm everyone. Blue to pink was easy enough, but we would need an angle on the pink to travel the 12 feet up the table to the final black and a 147 break – nothing was a certainty, especially as Jimmy himself knew he was on the verge of making history.

In truth, he butchered the blue. It went in but he was straight on the pink and didn't have any angle at all. He paused. JV called for hush. The only shot he had was a reverse deep screw off the opposite cushion to get anywhere near the black. If you're not a snooker player, let me put it this way: it was bloody near an impossible shot!

Jimmy threw everything at it, cue, shoulder, body, and the pot was made, part one... JV sprang into life as the cue ball started on its reverse-gear journey to the cushion.

'Go in, give us a chance... go on...'

The ball looked like it was slowing up, but once it hit the cushion, the side Jimmy had placed on the ball pinged it across the table. The black was makeable. One shot and we would all have witnessed the first-ever 147 from the break-off.

Those who have followed Jimmy's career closely will know that one black had already cost him a moment of history, in 1994 against Hendry. Ken, looking down from the balcony, had also suffered the agony of missing a final black at the 2000 Masters tournament for a maximum that would have yielded him an £80,000 sports car. Kirk and Cliff had known the feeling of making the 147; to be fair, so had Jimmy in 1992 against Drago.

We all held our breath. There was no money on offer, no sports car, not even a cheese sandwich, but none of that made this less important.

Jimmy nailed the black.

The place went wild and people were bouncing. Tornado Terry was more interested in knowing from JV if he got another frame!

We partied long into the night. Sure, Barcelona beat Man United 3-1 but no one seemed to really care! Plenty of the black stuff was consumed and Mr and Mrs Virgo did a duet with the band long into the early hours. We all had to remind ourselves that we had a show again the next day. It wasn't the first time the sun had started coming up before I'd gone to bed on a show night.

The story of Jimmy making the 147 from the break-off is now part of Legends history and although it gets mentioned a bit by Legends fans, I'm pretty sure anyone who has shared a pint or a pie at Dundalk FC with Tornado Terry since then has heard the story many more times.

We'll never know just how good a player 'Tornado Terry' was, and maybe that's how it should stay. He's part of snooker history, too!

CHAPTER 17

STEPHEN AND JIMMY

Stephen Hendry may well be the most decorated player in snooker history, but in a career where it's all about excelling as an individual, Stephen seems to really enjoy being part of our team.

Snooker Legends works because of the team ethic. It's not unusual when we are away on tour to find any of our players helping out during the day with the set-up of our show. Jimmy even grabs the hoover sometimes.

I think they almost enjoy spending the day in the venue creating the event, more than replicating the years of touring where if they weren't playing matches they would stare at hotel walls waiting for them to start. It's documented that Stephen's partner Lauren has worked for me for ten years, that they met on my show. They seem so well matched and so happy, she's definitely good for him.

We all work hard and play hard. We produce the very best show we can and then it's great as a team to relax and unwind afterwards over a pizza (Michaela Tabb's fault) and a beer, or in Stephen's case, the finest red wine the Premier Inn stocks!

In 2012 you would never before have seen a player more content with his retirement from professional snooker. Here is a man who sacrificed most of his childhood and adult life to be the very best at what he does; a ruthless winning machine. He simply got tired losing to people he felt were not worthy of sharing a table with him. I don't think Jimmy could have walked away quite so easily: the game runs through his veins.

Stephen played a huge part in creating the 'people's champion' tag Jimmy White now carries following the death of Alex. Seven times he won the titles and picked up the cheques; Jimmy won the fans and picked up the birds!

I've been privileged to spend time in the company of both of them and much as Jimmy wanted to win the World's, he is almost loved more, and therefore you could say he has earned more from the demand for exhibitions by not winning one.

It was Jimmy who got Stephen involved in year three of the tour. He set up a meeting for me at Alexandra Palace at the Masters. At the time Stephen was in the last year of his career, but no one knew it at that point. He shuffled into the players' room in a screwed-up check shirt, unshaven and wearing a flat cap. Think *Peaky Blinders'* Thomas Shelby but five years early. I assumed it was his day off... but he was in fact on his way to commentate!

We booked two shows, the first a clash at the Crucible with Jimmy, followed by a match at Preston Guildhall, another great snooker venue, two days later.

At that point, we knew the outcome of both their 2012 World Championship qualifiers would be known, or at least we thought so. Not for the first time, but I accept not on purpose, World Snooker changed the qualifying dates for the championship, so Jimmy and Stephen would have their final qualifying matches on our Preston date. I had to consider the fact that both would be battling for a place at the World Championship on the night I had sold 800 tickets for in Preston.

Thankfully, Freya at World Snooker reduced the risk for me by having both players play their final session of the match in the afternoon, but it still meant that if the match was close they would struggle to get to Preston on time.

Sadly Jimmy lost on the Thursday, and really having to stay for the Legends on the Friday night was torture, as it was the last place he wanted to be. But of course this Jimmy was very different from the one I'd first met in 2009 and there was no way he would let me down. The event had been sold out for weeks.

Stephen was drawn to play Yu Delu, a young Chinese player, and went 7-2 up in the first session race to 10 on the Saturday afternoon. This was good news as it meant that he only needed three frames for another World Championship appearance.

He rattled them off on the Sunday afternoon, jumped in his car and arrived in Preston 15 minutes before our VIP reception. Naturally he was buzzing, but he knew how much losing had meant to Jimmy, so he really contained himself. That showed real class; massive respect. Jimmy was the first to congratulate him, as well.

The Preston night went well and after the pack-up we returned to the hotel to find Stephen waiting up with drinks for everyone, including Jimmy. He immediately fitted in and obviously felt comfortable enough to confide in me that he was going to 'retire' at the Crucible in a week or so. At that point I think only his close family, Jimmy and I knew, so I suddenly felt a little humble to have been trusted with this secret.

I don't know if he was telling me to let me know he was free for work or whether he just felt comfortable sharing the news knowing there was still work to be had playing snooker with us in a more relaxed atmosphere after leaving the professional tour.

He also told us he had agreed a deal with JOY in China to launch their Chinese Black 8-ball pool game, which would see him over there playing Black 8 exhibitions on an almost monthly basis.

When the news broke, after he lost to Stephen Maguire, World

Snooker weren't happy. I even heard comments that they thought he had turned his back on the game that made him who he was. I don't think he owed them anything.

The reality was there were only four players left with any commercial value: Ronnie, of course, Steve Davis, Jimmy and Stephen. With Jimmy and Davis in a rankings free fall, and Ronnie firmly in 'may play'/'may not play' mode, they were losing an asset. It's sad they couldn't wish him well officially like his peers at the BBC did, with a guard of honour in the Crucible during the championship.

Of course he didn't retire quietly, just producing the tenth 147 of his career against Stuart Bingham, and then beating fellow Scot John Higgins before defeat to Maguire. It takes quite a lot to walk away when you've once again proved over the longer match format, under the intense pressure of a Crucible crowd, that you are still one of the top eight players in the world. I know that even if he had won it he was off. A new life beckoned.

Barry Hearn was never a Stephen Hendry fan, the real reason being that he was never able to manage or control him. I think Barry managed Jimmy about three or four times, probably sacking him for some misdemeanour and then being unable to say no when he wanted to come back, or he had a deal that required Jimmy to be a part of.

While Stephen dominated the game Barry had no choice, with regards to Matchroom matters, but to pander and work with Ian Doyle and his 110 Sport Management, who mentored and managed him.

Barry discovered Steve Davis, who won six world titles. Ian Doyle discovered Stephen, who won seven world titles. Barry was second best... ouch! Then again Barry had a chart hit with Snooker Loopy, which featured all the top players except Stephen and Parrott.

You could say Barry had the last laugh in 2010, as he bought the game and Ian Doyle and his 110 Sport Management went under.

I have no idea what Stephen gets paid in China – it's none of my business – but I do know it will be a damn sight more than I can ever pay him for a Legends show. He is treated like royalty out there, like a king: stays at the best hotels, eats at the top restaurants... In truth, luckily for me, he seems just as content with a takeaway pizza and a glass of red, which of course he will review on his wine app before consuming. Jimmy isn't fussy about hotels either; I think 20 years of probably meeting the breakfast waiter on his way to bed helps.

During his time as a professional player Jimmy has been popular with everyone, especially those who have a bit of work going. I don't think Stephen ever had a 'best mate' on tour; he was too interested in winning to care.

The closest person to him was, I believe, Mark Williams, now a three time world champion. Mark appeared in the very first year of Legends but hadn't appeared since, and was keen to do a show with Stephen. I set up a match at the Assembly Rooms in Derby for Stephen and Mark to take on Steve Davis and Jimmy. Mark is a wind-up merchant: on social media he is a master of being the cause of trouble or argument and then stepping away to avoid the flack. It works most of the time. It didn't work when he criticised the Crucible Theatre and received an £8,000 fine!

In the build-up to this event, Mark had stated on Twitter that if Stephen and he lost to Jimmy and Steve, he would have a tattoo done on his backside saying: 'I love Nugget'.

What was a flippant remark almost came back to haunt him big time as I made the very most of his tweet to get the maximum publicity. They did win, but not before a lot of drama where Stephen refused to take this impending date with the tattoo needle seriously. Twice on re-spotted blacks Stephen was trying to cut the ball in from the break. The normally confident Welsh Potting Machine was twitching for sure, not helped by Steve making buzzing sounds when he was down on the shot.

The great thing about Mark is that I have no doubt he would

have done it had they lost. He went naked for his press conference after winning in Sheffield this year, honouring a pledge. Mark is probably his closest friend in snooker but that doesn't mean Stephen won't take any opportunity to wind him up.

Moving forward, Stephen and Jimmy have a pivotal role in how the World Seniors Tour will develop. He showed me incredible loyalty in Germany when he saw I was being screwed over. I can't think there will have been many occasions in a career spanning 25 years that he has travelled overseas on a three-day playing trip and refused to take any payment for it?

He is hugely respected in the commentary team at the BBC; Jimmy is now part of the team at rival broadcaster Eurosport and now they fight over ratings not trophies.

I'd like to think people at Legends have already seen a different side of Stephen and Jimmy. I was honoured when they both accepted the captain's roles for the 2014 Legends Cup Team.

Jimmy's team slaughtered Stephen's. I guess the Whirlwind finally got some payback.

CHAPTER 18

THE TESTIMONIAL – JIMMY WHITE

In 2012 Jimmy White turned 50 years old; he also celebrated 30 years as a professional snooker player. Two good reasons to stage a testimonial – with the third, of course, being he could make himself some extra dough!

By the end of the 2011 tour we'd become close friends and although he had signed a management deal with Paul Mount at On Q Promotions, the reality was that Paul was never going to be able to manage Jimmy; he was more a figurehead for his new Snooker Academy in Gloucester.

Jimmy White is pretty much unmanageable. More than 35 years of being on the road have left him quite untrusting of some people – especially people within the game of snooker.

When he first asked me to organise a testimonial I was a bit taken aback, as really it was something his management team should have been doing. It was a huge challenge but one that I would relish. It was also one hell of a responsibility: he's a national treasure.

I knew Jimmy was loved, and I knew I could put on a good

event. It certainly didn't turn out as we both expected, but it was a great lesson for Jimmy in learning who his friends really were and it has seen me turn down two such requests to organise similar events for other players since.

I wanted at least a year to sort this. We ended up with nine months, and one testimonial in essence became two as we did a lunch and evening event – madness really, when I reflect upon it.

Our problem, which was actually a good problem to have, was that Ronnie O'Sullivan had agreed to play a snooker exhibition for Jimmy, and Ronnie Wood of the Rolling Stones had agreed to sing for him. Both offers were too good to turn down but there was no synergy between the two, even though of course Ronnie Wood is a huge snooker fan, and the two Ronnies and Jimmy have formed a formidable trio when out on the drink together.

The only answer was to stage two events: have a lunch with a snooker exhibition, then get rid of the snooker table and have a dinner and pop concert. Jimmy wanted to do it at the Grosvenor Hotel in London, in the Great Room. That immediately put the event under huge financial stress as hire costs alone were tens of thousands.

My idea was to invite every living World Snooker Champion along to host a table for Jimmy. It would help promote the event and give the fans a chance to meet a whole host of snooker stars. Spread the appeal.

Jimmy had shared the jungle with chef Gino D'Acampo and he agreed to design the menu for the two events; the cost alone was £50–£60 a head to us. I felt it was too much. Jimmy's fan base was more pie and mash, and here we were debating a drizzle of this and a smear of that. It felt a bit snobbish.

With every snooker champion bringing a guest and getting a complimentary room at the Grosvenor as a thank-you, we were already looking at a bill in excess of £50,000. I was worried, so called a meeting at Jimmy's house with his accountant, who was a fellow director of the testimonial committee, and Jimmy's daughter Lauren. I felt I needed help and contacts, and there was only one man for the job: Barry Hearn.

Jimmy phoned Barry and he agreed to come on board. I met with Barry two or three times and he helped set the table prices. He also bought two tables for Matchroom and gave us a great prize for the auction: tickets for a host of sporting events. He also allowed us to announce the event at the final of the 2011 Masters, but the BBC stopped that being broadcast, and the commentators were stopped from saying why Jimmy was in the audience that night. Petty really when you think how many viewers had tuned in to the BBC over the years because Jimmy was playing.

You could buy a 'Premier Table' hosted by a former World Snooker Champion for eight people for £8,000 all day, or £3,000 for lunch and £6,000 for dinner. You also got a signed cue from Jimmy. It seemed very expensive to me, with tickets averaging about £375 each. An 'Event Table' could sit ten: you didn't get the celebrity but you did get a cue. That was £5,000 for all day.

Looking back I think we should have just done the evening event with the Ronnie Wood concert. As much as people love seeing Ronnie O'Sullivan play snooker, you can pretty much see that at a Legends show.

From the very start people were only really interested in buying tables for the evening. Jimmy was staggered when a few of the world champions we'd invited presented us with bills for their flights. Sure it was only a couple hundred quid but it hurt him. Here was a man who had helped create the prize money in the 1980s; they had all got rich on it in the 1990s. He also remarked that he'd got at least a dozen exhibitions for each of these guys over the years and not asked for a penny.

After we launched at the Masters final I got about £30,000 pledged in tables. It was nothing really, and Jimmy and I endured six months of stress that we only shared between each other, trying to get people to commit.

Outwardly we proclaimed that bookings were going well, it

was going to be a great night and people needed to get their table secured. We had a minimum number set by the hotel, so if we didn't sell that number we'd be paying for those dinners anyway. While this was going on, Jimmy was also fighting for his place on tour as a professional snooker player, and his gout was flaring up again, making it painful to walk.

People who Jimmy had worked with for years suddenly couldn't make that night. Excuses like 'I'd like to, Jimmy, but business is slow' or 'Any weekend but that one, Jimbo' became a recurring theme. The simple fact was, Jimmy White fans were not the sorts of people to spend £375 on a meal at the Grosvenor Hotel.

The Grosvenor was the wrong place to stage it. That was partly my fault, but you couldn't really ask Ronnie Wood to play in a sports hall, could you? The event to celebrate one of the world's greatest-ever snooker players had to have some kudos, and Jimmy wanted a Central London location.

Because of the pressure of not selling tables, we had no money to spend on the event itself. I cut together a 20-minute DVD from footage showing the highlights of Jimmy's career; it was acceptable but certainly not professional. I really could have done with being able to use some of Barry's production team at Matchroom. We tried to get memorabilia on show, like Jimmy's jungle uniform, and he agreed to auction basically everything he had. I got my designer to print off some nice photographs from his career.

We really were trying to make it look good, but everything now had to be about making as much money from the people who were attending the event, as it was obvious we weren't going to sell all the tickets.

In January I first made contact with the Rolling Stones' office. Obviously having Ronnie Wood play was going to need some organising. Up to this point, though, Jimmy and I thought that it would be Ronnie sat on a stool with an acoustic guitar.

What we ended up with was far bigger and better, but it no longer came for free! Shirley at the Stones' office told me that Ronnie was putting together a band for the night and they had all agreed to play for free. Amazing, I thought, especially when we were told that Ronnie would be joined on stage by fellow Stones Bill Wyman and Mick Taylor, and the front man would be no other than Mick Hucknall from Simply Red.

Ronnie Wood's son, Jesse, was going to work with me on logistics and it soon became clear that although the band would perform for free, the bill for all the rehearsals, their personal expenses, studio hire, and all the sound and light costs were going to have to be picked up by Jimmy himself from the testimonial income!

Jimmy felt too embarrassed to tell Ronnie Wood. I was also told by Shirley that all the band members, except Ronnie, had to be given £1,000 in cash in an envelope on the night to cover their expenses.

One minute I was being told how lucky we were to have Mick Hucknall playing, as he usually charged £150,000 per appearance, and the next thing I'm being told to stuff an envelope with £1,000 as Mick's about to get his taxi and wants his expenses! The bloke could sing, but aside from that he was pretty unpleasant to all my team. I could certainly find better ways to spend 150,000 quid, that's for sure.

To cut a long story short, Ronnie Wood's involvement in the testimonial cost us about £20,000, save some change. While the joint rocked, and people danced to some of rock and roll's biggest legends, only Jimmy and I knew the full picture. We paid for everything from the 24 cans of Red Bull in the green room for the band, right down to a driver and amp for Bill Wyman. Thank God most of them were reformed alcoholics and no longer drinking or it could have been even worse.

The other issue was that although all of Jimmy's so-called friends were not able to buy tables and tickets to support him, they were able to come out of the woodwork to ask for free ones. On top of the tickets for the snooker players who were hosting tables, we did a free table for his manager Paul and his sponsor – no problem at all with any of that.

However, the whole lunch became farcical as people turned up on the door asking for Jimmy and trying to get in for free. I was furious: this was the Grosvenor Hotel not some bloody exhibition in Tooting.

Also, logistically, we had a meticulous table plan. Jimmy was being made to let people in, and chairs were being pulled up to tables with guests asking for place settings. Much as I would love to name names in here, it wouldn't be fair to Jimmy. He knows exactly who turned up, and the extra £3,000 he spent buying dinners for freeloaders and 'old friends' didn't get forgotten. Many 'old friends' probably think it's weird that they no longer hear from Jimmy, or why he no longer takes their calls. It was disgusting.

Also, originally planned for the night was impressionist and singer Joe Longthorne, another friend of Jimmy's. The plan was that after dinner Joe would go on and get the crowd going, and then we'd do the auction before Ronnie Wood played.

Also, for reasons I will never understand, Jimmy had asked an amateur Elvis tribute act to close the night. I pleaded with him to just get a DJ in, and Barry Hearn knew DJ Spoony, but Jimmy had asked 'The King of Rock 'n' Roll' in a drunken moment at a previous show and felt he couldn't disappoint the lad.

To be fair, following Ronnie Wood and Mick Hucknall was never going to be easy, but this guy and his band were nothing more than average, and this was far and away the biggest gig they had ever played – it was a bit embarrassing and the dance floor was empty. 'Burning Love' it was certainly not – more 'Suspicious Minds'!

We had some fantastic auction items: a cue painted by Damien Hirst and a round of golf in Florida donated by Ian Poulter.

Messrs Wood, Hucknall and Wyman also signed guitars, one of which was given to talkSPORT's Andy Goldstein for hosting the event.

But I had a problem. Joe Longthorne was ill the night before the show. So without Joe, I either went straight to the auction after dinner, which felt a bit mercenary, or we let them have Ronnie Wood, get them up dancing and feeling like they had a great night, and then hit them with a chance to spend.

I put Ronnie Wood on. It was a big call, and Barry said, 'Great night, Jason, but you've fucked your auction.' The truth is, I think there was only a certain amount of money in the room and we would have got it either way. Barry was probably right though.

Willie Thorne did the auction for Jimmy. Undoubtedly there was no one better for the job and to raise the maximum amount of money.

It was an amazing night for Jimmy and his family, and it did celebrate him turning 50 and having 30 years in the game. Sadly it didn't really make Jimmy any money, but he found out who his friends really were.

I speak to Jimmy every day; he's one of my best friends in the sport. Reading his recent book, cleverly titled *Second Wind*, I don't know the man who talks about what he did in the 1980s and 1990s. I can certainly believe it, but it's not the bloke I know to be one of my best friends today.

He says he's wasted about four million on gambling, drink, drugs and having a good time. For a man who lived in a world of cash exhibitions I reckon it's nearer double that.

Jimmy thinks he is a changed man because he has not taken cocaine for 20 years and that he hardly ever has a drink. With mobile phones, cameras and social media he certainly could never get away in the modern era with what he did in the old days. We often laugh about what Alex Higgins would have been like on Twitter or Facebook – absolute mayhem.

One of Jimmy's top qualities is his generosity. If I was ever in trouble he would be my first call, and I know he would do whatever he could to help me.

Sadly, I know the day when Jimmy White no longer plays professional snooker is not too far away; he's got an Invitational Wild Card currently, but that will expire. I have no idea how he will cope with that, but if I can get it right, the World Seniors Tour will be there waiting for him.

Jimmy can be found in life's dictionary under the description 'No Regrets'. Asked if he would do it all again the same way, he simply says, 'What do you think?' The Whirlwind may not blow quite as hard as it once did but he will be forever regarded as part of snooker's royalty.

Those South London roots will never completely go away; Jimmy is always looking for a deal, an angle, a swerve. He must be the director or shareholder in a hundred companies, many of which promised him millions and ended up bankrupt. He's been a drug taker, a drinker, a gambler, bankrupt and a bad husband... He's also a great father, a generous friend, raised thousands for charity and done more free shows for good causes than I care to remember. He never turns down an autograph or a photo, although it is fair to say he'd prefer to sell you one of his.

I've seen him up after winning matches and down after getting beaten – sadly he gets beaten more than he wins these days and the hurting gets worse. He won the UK Seniors Championship with me in 2017, his teenage son stood proudly at the trophy presentation with him. I think it was probably something he thought would never happen; he had that winning feeling again.

Mention the name Jimmy White to people on the street and they immediately smile. He has that effect on people. He has that effect on me.

CHAPTER 19

LIVERPOOL IN OCTOBER

During Ronnie's 'retirement from professional snooker' we planned an October 2012 tour of six Legends shows and didn't just talk about creating our own 'Ronnie challenges...' series. The issue of forming a breakaway association from World Snooker began taking shape.

Even though Ronnie was adamant he was not going to play again, I was still not going to start booking theatres for shows that clashed with the major tournaments in the calendar. If history had taught me anything, I knew that Ronnie could be guilty of the odd change of mind!

He had left Grove Leisure and signed a contract with Merlin Entertainments. Merlin was the management company of cricketer Freddie Flintoff and former footballer Jamie Redknapp. Ronnie had met them whilst appearing as a guest on the Sky comedy panel show *A League of Their Own*. The idea was that Merlin were going to help develop his media career away from snooker, and we were going to carry on working directly, like we always had, on the Legends shows.

People say Ronnie is difficult to manage, and they point to the number of managers he has gone through during his career as proof of this. People like Django at Grove have successfully managed Judd Trump and Neil Robertson, and in the early days Ronnie was managed by Barry Hearn himself. Those two could argue that they are proven managers of successful players.

Generally players pay a percentage of their table earnings to their managers; to my knowledge Ronnie never has. His argument, and it's a valid one, is that they cannot affect what he does on the table, so why should they share in that income?

Sure, if we are providing an administration service, or coming to events to assist, booking hotels, then I believe it should not be costing us, we should get paid and looked after.

The opportunity for Ronnie's agent to earn comes from the off-table commercial deals, or the logo patches they can deliver because of who Ronnie is and what he has won on the table. However, having Ronnie O'Sullivan in your stable means you will attract other players to your management who *will* pay you a percentage of tournament winnings.

What I do disagree with, and what I believe has happened with previous managers in the past, is to use a commercial approach for Ronnie and divert it to another player you manage because you'll earn a higher percentage from the deal you have with them.

Ronnie has the occasional 'mad' moment. For example, he signed an exclusive management deal with Merlin without even reading the contract, or getting someone else to read it. Just as he does with his game, he lives on instinct, using a sixth sense of right and wrong. But contracts are 25 pages for a reason, and not for the first time, when Ronnie decided he no longer wanted to be with Merlin, he found the contract clauses were going to make a divorce pretty expensive.

In about September 2012 we did a show in Ipswich, and Ronnie told me the contract issues were sorted and he was going to play a bit again. He entered a small PTC Event in Gloucester and the International Tournament in China.

The last date of our tour was going to be played in Liverpool, a town very dear to Ronnie, where he lived for a couple of years when he first was turning pro. The tournament snooker attendances, particularly the Premier League Snooker on Sky, were suffering because Ronnie wasn't in it. While we packed in 1,500 people at the Echo Arena in Liverpool, the Premier League match in Guildford, live on Sky with Bingham and Ebdon, had about a hundred attending, with many of them being free tickets given out to local clubs. I knew this wouldn't go down well with World Snooker and that was the last year Sky broadcast the Premier League.

While I was working alongside the theatre to help promote our show, we got the chance to do some advertising with Liverpool and Everton Football Clubs. It was also made clear that if I could get Ronnie to go and visit the training grounds, as a bit of pre-publicity, then we would get lots of local newspaper coverage. I am a massive Liverpool fan, so the chance to visit Melwood and rub shoulders with Gerrard and Carragher was a dream come true. The only day that would work was in between our shows in Ipswich and Bedworth, and the only time slot we could get was 10am.

I checked the map. It was 245 miles, easily four and a half hours. I knew I had no chance of getting Ronnie to get up at 4am and let me drive him to Liverpool to shake a few Scousers' hands; he has no interest in football to start with, and even I knew it was a big ask. So I started to give Jimmy the blather about how ticket sales were slow in Liverpool, and we had this great chance to go up to the football grounds to help with the marketing.

He saw straight through me. 'If this is about you wanting to kiss Gerrard's arse, then just say so and ask me properly!'

'OK, Jimmy, will you get in a car with me at 4am, let me drive you to Liverpool to both training grounds and then let me drive you back to Bedworth for our next show?'

Silence...

'Are you fucking kiddin' me?' he said, then he smiled. 'Of course I will...' And so the deal was done. Well, at least part of it. I just had to convince Everton and Liverpool now that it would be Jimmy coming, not Ronnie. They weren't keen!

Luckily for us, Brendan Rodgers, the Liverpool manager at the time, was a snooker fan; in fact he had met Jimmy at Chelsea when he was working with José Mourinho. The gig was on, and for once my Snooker Legends show had opened the door for me to meet my footballing heroes. It wasn't lost on me that the enthusiasm I had was similar to that experienced by snooker fans coming through our doors to meet our players.

Jimmy had no problem getting up. He was waiting for me, and we actually left early. OK, he did sleep most of the way but fair play to him. We were due to visit Everton first. To be honest I wasn't that bothered with 'The Toffees' personally but I understood this was a marketing exersise not about my personal football preference, but the facilities at Finch Farm were amazing, and we got to chat to the boys who had just come back from international duty and were in having a rub-down.

David Moyes was charming, liked his snooker and knew John Parrott well; in fact John's sister-in-law is married to Toffee legend Duncan Ferguson who was working on the staff at the time with the reserve team. He's now with the first team and probably destined to get the top job one day. We gave Moyes a signed cue and got out of there as soon as we could; I wanted as much time at Melwood as possible!

As we entered through the gates to the Liverpool training facility, Jimmy said I was quiet. I was thinking back to all my heroes who had basically 'come to work' here every day. Emlyn Hughes, King Kenny, John Barnes and, of course, Stevie G.

As England had been playing overseas the night before, I

wasn't even sure Gerrard would be in, but the first player we met, Carra, confirmed he was, and said he'd go and tell him we had a cue for him.

We watched them train a bit from their canteen. They had a couple of 8-ball tables but they were in a terrible condition. All the guys came in and we got our photos. We gave Stevie a cue and Jimmy had a game with Carra and Joe Cole, who he knew from Chelsea.

Brendan Rodgers was charming and invited us into his office for a cuppa, with his assistant Colin Pascoe. We gave Brendan a nice piece of memorabilia signed by Ronnie; in return we got a signed ball and Jimmy got a shirt. Stevie was a snooker fan: he'd had a full-size in his house but found it too tricky, so had a 9-foot table put in instead. Sadly, fixtures meant none of the first team would be able to come on the night of our actual show, but it was still a thrill being there. While there, Jimmy promised to get them a 9-ball table. I sorted it, and when it did arrive it was a beauty, red cloth with the 'JFT 96' (Justice for the Hillsborough 96) logo on it.

One funny incident did occur while we were in the manager's office. I couldn't help but notice all the self-help books on the shelves, and of course the Steve Peters book, *The Chimp Paradox*. It was obvious Brendan was a scholar. He said that he always liked to pass one piece of advice to his players from any top sportsman who visited Melwood. In Jimmy's case he was really impressed with how Jimmy had lost all those major finals with Hendry, yet kept picking himself up and coming back for more.

Brendan asked him how he managed to do that, what his thought process was, his pen and notebook poised for some Whirlwind wisdom he could pass onto the Liverpool legends. To be honest, the answer he got wasn't going to rewrite any motivational book soon.

'Jimmy, I'm a huge fan, how did you deal with losing those finals to Hendry?'

Jimmy put his coffee down.

'Well if I'm gonna be honest, Brendan, I was pissed for the first two, got battered in the next one, and my arse fell out on the black in the last one...'

Brendan put down the pen and reached for the chocolate digestives. I think it's fair to say no pearls of wisdom were coming his way that day – unless of course, being a Chelsea fan, Jimbo didn't want to reveal his secrets!

Ronnie's flight to China was from Heathrow the morning after our Liverpool show. Django had organised a car for Ronnie but we had organised a night out in Liverpool to end our tour.

First Ronnie said, 'I got to fly off straight after the show.'

Then it changed to: 'I'll stay for an hour or so, we'll get some food.'

Then, after the third vodka and orange, to him breaking down and saying, 'I don't wanna go China, Jase, I can't do it.'

I was pretty speechless. The criticism about his walking away from snooker the previous May had all died down, and the positive media were reporting how great it was that he was coming back to play again. They were going to crucify him for this change of heart and I did worry that the Legends Tour would get blamed.

He was suffering with his back: we'd had to get him painkillers during our tour, and I think that was the official reason for his withdrawal as he had been worried about the long flight. I think the truth was he was scared about the flight and what the pressure of his comeback and playing again would do to him. He'd been rushed back before he was ready and the demons were telling him to run away again: it was the easier option for him. Ronnie's dad was with us in Liverpool and like any caring father was telling him to do what he felt was right, not to feel pressured into going to China if he wasn't ready.

We all went out to the Marriott Hotel; it was Les and Bobby's birthday, two guys known to the players on the snooker scene.

Tony Knowles was there as well, someone who had worked on some of my shows in 2011.

Tony, Ronnie and I were chatting – actually I lie, because Tony was chatting and we were listening! (John Parrott tells a story of the flight to Australia back in the 1980s when he decided an hour into the 12-hour trip to Singapore to go and sit alongside Tony for a chat. He asked him one question about rankings and another about the governing body, and he said the next thing he knew he heard the announcement to fasten seatbelts as they were coming in to land. Tony likes a chat, that's for sure.)

By this time Ronnie's mind was made up. The car had been cancelled and his room stay extended at the hotel. I knew there would be a backlash the next morning.

With Ronnie still in retirement but playing Legends shows, we were getting some negative publicity, more I think frustration from snooker fans in general, who couldn't understand that he was OK to play exhibitions with Jimmy but not enter main events.

The deadline for the UK Championship came and went, then he turned down his right to play in the Masters, leaving one final question: Would Ronnie return to Sheffield to defend his World Championship?

With not playing or getting a single ranking point, Ronnie was now ranked world number 29, which would have meant that he had to win qualifying matches in the Sports Hall to even get to the Crucible.

However, because he had won the World Championship in 2012, there is a rule that for the next season the holder is automatically seeded 1 for the next World's, or 2 at any other event behind the defending champion. It was a perfect scenario as he really could play when he wanted to.

In January 2013 we met up for some dinner. 'If you can get me the right deal, Jase, I'll enter the World's.'

CHAPTER 20

THE RETURN OF THE ROCKET

At the time I got the green light to try and make getting him to play in the 2013 World Snooker Championship happen, Ronnie was still with Merlin but they hadn't delivered anything and the Rocket realised that he wasn't quite ready to hang up his cue for good.

We kept it quiet at the time; to be fair there was nothing to tell. I only confided in Jimmy White, who had just started work with the ROK Group, who were launching a new vodka called Oval.

Ronnie also wanted me to get him a cue deal. It was complete nonsense that the world champion wasn't endorsing, and therefore earning from, the sale of snooker cues with his name on it.

I found a deal with BCE Riley, but they wanted five years and at the time Ronnie couldn't commit to playing for that long. In 2014, two years later, he signed the five-year deal with them, I missed out on any commission from the deal.

I formulated a plan with Jimmy that if he could get ROK boss Jonathan Kendrick (always known as JK) to a hotel in the West End then I'd get Ronnie there and we'd try to do a deal.

Ronnie had given me a figure he wanted. It was significant and I explained that no one would pay him that amount for one tournament, especially when he hadn't played for 12 months and could get knocked out on Day 1. They might, however, if he committed to play ten events the following season.

On the flip side I was emailing ROK saying that this would be headline news: not only would they get exposure from him playing at the World Championship, where the defending champion always opens proceedings, but also from a news conference I could arrange with BBC, Sky and ITV. I was overplaying the deal for ROK and underplaying it to Ronnie. God knows why, as I had nothing to gain financially.

Jimmy got JK to London and I persuaded Ronnie to come and meet him. JK's background was motor racing; he had made his fortune as an importer of Yokohama tyres, supplying people like the late Ayrton Senna and Eddie Jordan. His wide ROK Star portfolio of companies included oil, water, security systems, mobile phones, energy drinks, beer and the new vodka.

We stayed about an hour. The deal was done in five minutes with a handshake – the rest of the time was spent discussing their mutual love of motor racing. The deal was easy; keeping the deal quiet and arranging the press conference was not!

We had until 27th February to confirm his entry for the 2013 World Championship; we decided to do the press conference on the 26th, taking it right to the edge for maximum impact. I started working with a marketing guy at ROK called Bruce. He was great and it was like we were planning a clandestine special-forces raid, which, seeing as he was a former tank commander in the army, was quite ironic.

On 5th February we did a Legends event in Ireland, with Ronnie and Steve Davis. Even Steve was asking Ronnie if he was going to play in the World's. Rather than deny it or lie to the Nugget, Ronnie simply said he hadn't decided what he was doing.

We wanted to get a Central London hotel, and we ended up

with the Hilton Metropole in Edgware. It wasn't ideal and I was very worried that we wouldn't get the press and I'd end up with egg on my face.

In the interim we had paid off Merlin. They earned a significant sum of money from Ronnie for printing off a contract. He could have fought it but he just wanted to take the financial pain and move on. Over the years Ronnie has refurbished a few lawyers' offices with his legal fees and I think it just wears him down.

For this press conference I got my PR lady, Debbie, on it and we released a statement. I wanted to dangle the carrot but also not give it away. I must have done a dozen different drafts, but in the end it simply said:

> '*Current World Snooker Champion Ronnie O'Sullivan has called a press conference on Tuesday 26th February to make a statement to the press and clarify his future career plans.*'

I'd confided in only one other person, talkSPORT presenter Andy Goldstein. Andy had hosted Jimmy's testimonial for me and we'd become friends when meeting at the Sky events. He was snooker mad and even played at the show in Brighton for us as our special guest.

Andy went to school with Ronnie; I think he was a couple of years above him. He does the late show on talkSPORT, getting in at about 2am; he also fronts some of the Eurosport Snooker Coverage. Don't feel sorry for him – he has his dream job! However, that said, I didn't want to drag him from his home after a few hours' sleep for him to hear Ronnie roll out his 'I'm retiring' speech.

The news was going to be confirmed by the first line of my statement. Andy had already typed the tweet and he hit the send button the moment I said it – he was the first to release the news to the sporting world.

We'd got Sky there, BBC and ITV; it was a huge relief. Jimmy was coming as well – he was now a ROK Ambassador.

I picked Ronnie up about 10am; he was wearing ripped jeans and a shirt. For once I had to advise it wasn't appropriate. He'd packed a pair of black trousers and a jacket and we had to get the team in London to rush out for a waistcoat and white shirt.

I smuggled him into the hotel, and we chilled out in the room so he could change as the world's sports press were assembling downstairs. Ronnie's World Trophy was also making an appearance, alongside the Oval Vodka brand of course, which he would soon be promoting.

It was from this day that I took on my first tenure as Ronnie's kind of manager – well, maybe not manager, more organiser. It was a role I probably could have taken on full-time on two other occasions but it was one I shied away from because of my friendship with him. I only did it full-time from 2015.

Commercially, earning commission from him was easy, certainly not rocket science. Companies were coming to him to spend their money, but I didn't want to be the guy dealing with any issues or problems with World Snooker, or telling him off for not signing autographs for fans. At that time, I was happy to help out 'unofficially' up to the World's but not beyond that.

Of course history shows that he went on to win the championship so my managerial record started with one tournament, one victory, one World Championship! Should have stopped there really.

One thing I did miss in the chaos of the press conference was a courtesy call to Barry Hearn and Jason Ferguson. I felt this was important, but of all the places in the world you could get a mobile phone service, it seemed the Metropole in Edgware was not one of them. I did get through to them both just after the conference but that was wrong really. They should have been told beforehand. Of course Barry was ecstatic; the price for the eventual tournament sponsor Betfair probably went up straight after the call!

Very few people thought Ronnie could take a year off the sport and come back and win it. There weren't really any comparisons in sport to judge it on. Sure, in boxing a fighter may not fight for a year, but he is training and sparring.

Apart from his Legends shows, Ronnie had not been playing; his cue was being stored at his mum's. He knew it was a huge challenge, but he also knew he had eight weeks to prepare and it was perfect motivation for him.

Ronnie went live on Sky News, Radio 5 Live and ITV. We got loads of tabloid coverage the next day, and part one of the job was done. I felt proud to have got it this far.

I was away working when Ronnie had to go to do the publicity day. Barry Hearn was sat there, centre stage; Mark Selby was suited and booted; and Ronnie was in a hoodie looking completely disinterested in it all. It didn't look great to be honest.

Betfair had designed a gold cue for any maximum break. They did a photo shoot with Ronnie in his hoodie looking down the cue. It was like a cover for the computer game *Assassin's Creed* – very bizarre.

The build-up to Sheffield was crazy and the pressure was telling on him. I needed to do his logo, and ROK had discussed using a different one for each session to get publicity for more than just one of the brands. It was a good idea and actually something Jimmy had been doing for years, although in Jimmy's case he'd had to do it when he sold two logo patches at an event when you could only wear one! People kept asking if he had a water problem as he seemed to be visiting the toilet after every frame. What they didn't know was it was like Mr Benn in the bog as he switched waistcoats each time – that's Jimmy!

However, there was a problem. The world champion only had one waistcoat. Unbelievable really. Like saying Tiger Woods only has one golf shirt.

Historically the BBC coverage would start at 1pm on the first day and start with a review of the morning's play when the defending champion would begin his campaign. The return of the Rocket meant that BBC were going live at 10am. JK and ROK were delighted: huge viewing figures were guaranteed.

I arrived in Sheffield on the Friday afternoon. Ronnie was at his usual hotel and I went down to get his waistcoat to put the logo on. I caught him coming back from the physio: he'd pulled his hamstring running; it was the first of many injuries that would blight him over the coming years.

I wasn't invited up to his room to collect the waistcoat. He brought it down and then arranged with me to bring it to the Crucible the next morning. It felt a bit strange, and I knew Damien was in town, but I'd assumed I'd be at least spending some time with him. Had I offended him?

I didn't expect to be sewing on the vodka logo sat in the foyer of the Hilton hotel, especially as I was surrounded by boxer Audley Harrison, who was fighting in Sheffield the following night, and his entourage. Goodness knows what I looked like sat there with my thimble on amongst these pugilists!

I also had some more aggravation around an advertising deal I had done with Programme Master, the company who had the contract to sell space in the official World Championship brochure. I'd been taking a few adverts out with them across the year at the major snooker tournaments, and also took one in the West Ham United programme when we had a gig in Essex. This time they had a great deal: as well as a page in the programme, I could appear in the digital copy on the World Snooker website with a link to my Snooker Legends app, the topic of my advert. I also asked if I could display a pop-up banner in the foyer of the Crucible. The footfall across the 17 days there is huge and a nice banner advertising my app, which was free to download, would be hitting my target audience. 'No problem,' said Programme Master; we were a loyal partnership.

I guess at this point no one thought to check with the commercial director at World Snooker, the bloke I'd had an uneasy relationship with over the Eurosport issue, to make sure it was OK to have a competitor's brand plonked in the middle of the Crucible concourse during the World Championship. Either that or he missed exactly who this deal had been done with. I duly dropped off my banner on the Friday to a guy called Simon; I just knew that once it went up in full view, someone was not going to be pleased. But I'd done the deal, signed the contract and paid my money.

I quickly learned that the World Championship, and the expectation and pressure, brought out a very different side in Ronnie. His best mate, Irish Chris, had arrived and I got the impression that the inner circle for the World's would be limited to him and Damien Hirst. Of course now that I have been in that inner circle with Ronnie and Damien in Sheffield I understand far better the dynamic and realise it wasn't personal.

There was no real issue, but here I was paying for my own hotel room and fuel to Sheffield. Perhaps Ronnie assumed ROK were paying for it and maybe ROK felt that Ronnie was paying it. Who knows? I never mentioned it.

I walked down to the Crucible with JV that morning. There was a real buzz in the air. Crowds were gathering at the stage door but Ronnie never uses it, preferring to avoid the crowd by diving through the gap in the security fence.

By sheer coincidence, as I reached the corner so did Damien's car with Ronnie in it. He saw me and took me through with him. I carried the waistcoat to his dressing room and so started a weird superstition for a couple of years of me always delivering his waistcoat on Day 1 of a major.

We did it in Sheffield that year, he won; we did it at the Masters and he won. We also did it at the World's in 2014 and he was runner-up – but as Meatloaf says, 'Two out of three ain't bad'.

After leaving Ronnie to prepare for his opening match with

Marcus Campbell I walked round to the front to make sure my banner was up. It wasn't. I chased down Simon and he awkwardly said Miles Pearce, World Snooker's commercial director, wouldn't let it go up. 'Too late,' I said, waving the conveniently placed contract I had in his face. 'I've signed a contract. I suggest you take that to Miles and get the banner up straight away.'

This was the morning of Ronnie's comeback, and the place was heaving. The banner did eventually go up, but not until after the first day. Maybe Miles felt he had some sort of victory in stopping me advertising on the opening day of the championship. All I know is I had 16 more days of it up and got all my money back from Programme Master.

Because of work I didn't go for the second round or quarters, but I was back for the semi-final against Judd. Ronnie was getting stronger as each game went on, and people were beginning to believe that he could achieve the impossible.

Judd would be a different proposition to the others; he was the young kid on the block. He'd reached the final in 2011, won a few tournaments and was driving round in a Ferrari. He'd also started wearing shoes that apparently cost £2,000 but made him look like he was treading on a pair of hedgehogs.

But once Ronnie got in front he never looked back, and won quite easily. Judd dispatched, the opponent for the final was Barry Hawkins. To many the job was done, and beating Barry, who was reaching his first final, would just be a formality. No such thoughts from Ronnie; he was far too experienced to think that. We were so close, but still so far away, well 18 frames to be exact...

CHAPTER 21

THE 2013 FINAL

It had always been a tradition at major finals for Ronnie's kids, mum and sister to appear for the final session and usually the trophy pictures, but this time there was a problem. Unbeknown to Ronnie, and intentionally kept from him, his mum Maria was pretty unwell. I knew she had been to hospital for tests but I didn't know what for. It was pretty serious but she was adamant that her son shouldn't know.

Ronnie started the match better and took the first two frames, but Barry then took the next three and for the first time in the championship Ronnie was trailing in a match. Back against the wall, he went super-aggressive, rattling off two centuries, 133 and 103, and led the final 5-3 after the first session. I always wondered whether Barry Hawkins believed he could beat Ronnie to become a World Snooker Champion. Had he already missed his opportunity?

Barry Hawkins came back in the evening and drew level at 7-7. It showed great character to win four of the first six with the crowd heavily supporting the rocket. A break of 103 in the

15th frame was Ronnie's 128th century break at the World Championship, breaking another of Hendry's records.

Just as he had done in patches throughout the event, he found another gear and rolled off the last two frames of the day to take a 10-7 overnight lead. That was crucial; for me Barry's race was run.

Maria didn't think she would be well enough to attend the final day and knew that she'd have to tell her son that morning; she couldn't avoid the question any longer. Early on Monday Damien Hirst had sent his personal driver to collect Ronnie Junior from Essex, the plan to get him back for 1pm regardless of his whether his mum travelled or not. With Ronnie 10-7 up in the match overnight it was odds on that he was going to win his fifth world title in the most remarkable of circumstances.

I'd spoken with Maria at about 5pm the day before. She wanted to be there but there was no way she was strong enough to drive. I offered to come and get her. I felt it was important. I lost my mum at just 28 years old; you only get one mum. How I was actually going to do that, I wasn't quite sure.

Late that night I drove back home from Sheffield, it was the only way: 250 miles, three coffees, and a 1am arrival. I was shattered. At 6am I set off again, this time to Chigwell to collect Maria and her friend Sinead, two hours and more coffee, plus some mints! Then we started the three-hour trip to Sheffield itself. I'd done five hours and about 350 miles to get everyone to the Crucible to find that there were only two passes left on the door. I gave them to Maria and Sinead.

I did feel a little sorry for myself, and a little angry, but Rachel at World Snooker got me a ticket, so I was able to watch, although to be truthful I was falling asleep.

Ronnie knew his mum was watching but he had no idea how she'd got there or that she wasn't well. He's never asked and I've never told him. I'm very close to Maria; she's typically Sicilian, quite fiery but always with some grub on the go! No fool in business either, her property company with her son is substantial. I think the family home is a welcome sanctuary for Ronnie, somewhere he goes to escape.

Ronnie led 15 frames to 10 after the afternoon games, dominating the third session with heavy scoring. He went on to win the final 18-12 to take his fifth world title and create that fairy-tale ending.

At the age of 37, he became the oldest World Snooker Champion since 45-year-old Ray Reardon in 1978. When he paraded the trophy round he came to the area we were standing and offered it up. It was a nice touch to think he acknowledged I'd played a very small part in helping it happen.

Without me getting him the ROK deal would he have entered at all? We will never know, but history shows that Ronnie O'Sullivan took a year out of the sport and came back to defend his World Championship. Typical O'Sullivan.

CHAPTER 22

THE LEGENDS CUP, YEAR ONE – DAY 1

I don't watch a lot of golf these days, I play even less, but I've always been a huge fan of the Ryder Cup, so when I heard Dennis, Cliff and JP talking about how much they used to enjoy the snooker team events, it got me thinking.

Snooker used to have a team event called the Nations Cup, an invitational snooker tournament created in 1999. The event featured teams of four players representing their country against others but it was purely singles with rotating match-ups. It was staged at a time when snooker was really popular and it offered a nice alternative to the regular one-on-one matchplay, as, to be fair, did the Hoffmeister World Doubles! The first winners of the Nations Cup were Wales with a team of Mark Williams, Matthew Stevens, Dominic Dale and Darren Morgan. The event only lasted until 2001, although I don't think we can blame God's country for its demise.

By 2012 I was already in a position to pretty much stage whatever I wanted. I had all the players on board now, including Ronnie, and I thought it was time to offer up something different for the Legends fans. My issue of course was financing it. By having eight players at an event, the wage bill was going to rise.

I first discussed the idea with JP. He thought it was great and I shared my vision: again four players would represent their countries, like the Nations Cup, but they'd be playing doubles and singles with a point per match. Each of the first three sessions would have two doubles matches and then four singles, with the final session being all singles. Again, does that format remind you of anything? Singles were one-frame shoot-outs but with the doubles I made them best of three. However, if it was 1-1 then we just put the black up for a re-spot instead of playing out the third frame, which would mean there was drama every step of the way.

I also wanted the event to be settled in a dramatic fashion, so decided that the winning post should be 18 points. JP thought that was too much: 'Make it 14 like the Ryder Cup,' he said. He also pointed out that it was pretty tough for one team to get to 18 when the format I was suggesting only offered up 26 in total over the four sessions.

But that was my point. I didn't want a team to get to 18 in normal play. I wanted to stage a dramatic finish by playing out the 26 points and then having all players in the arena facing off with black ball re-spots. It should mean that at the point of victory all the players were out there with the fans, ecstasy in one corner and devastation in the other.

At the end of the day it was still an exhibition with players getting appearance money, but I needed to add an edge. It had to matter, otherwise those emotions I was trying to conjure up would never be real. I owed it to the fans to put on an event where all the players would be trying as hard as they normally would in a ranking tournament.

JP said, 'Put a bit of prize money on it to make us try – but not too much so you lose the entertainment feel of your event.' It was great advice.

The idea of a two-day Legends Cup was born. Now all I needed was a venue to support it that could minimise my financial risk. After all, just because I thought it was a good idea, and one snooker player did as well, that didn't guarantee it was going to work, did it?

My saviour came by way of an unlikely location but one which had a manager who shared my ambition. His name was Tim Norton and the venue was Bedworth Civic Hall. 'Where?' you ask. I know it was hardly the Crucible or Alexandra Palace, but it was ideal for a number of reasons.

Bedworth is a market town near Nuneaton in the Midlands. It's about 20 miles east of Birmingham, and 15 miles northeast of Warwick. Nobody could argue it wasn't central. What Bedworth offered me was a theatre manager who was keen to put his venue on the map for major sporting events. He had tried to get snooker before, and almost got the Sky Premier League, but the hall was a few feet too small for the camera runs.

Because the council had shared this vision they were prepared to guarantee me a fee for bringing the Legends Cup to their venue, plus we had a local hotel, Weston Hall, that would provide free accommodation for the players. It was a huge project, but because of the support from Nuneaton Council it was relatively low financial risk for me.

I wanted to work with the players who were already in the team. I felt loyal to them, and so I needed to take some artistic licence with the teams. My captains were going to be Dennis and Cliff, two foes from as early as 1973 when they first played each other. I knew they would take it seriously, and beating each other as captain of their teams would mean as much as beating each other in a major-ranking final.

I also needed to include Jimmy, Ronnie and JP, so a team of England and Northern Ireland was created. It was in theory the UK without Wales and Scotland – I'd already created my own devolution far in advance of what Alex Salmond tried to do in 2014!

Thinking about Cliff as captain of the other team, I knew it couldn't just be drawn from Canada. At the end of the day, Cliff was 65 years old, a pensioner, but still their best player. The opposition needed to be competitive as the England and Northern Ireland team had the current World Snooker Champion, Ronnie, on it. I wanted to use Stephen Hendry as well, so the easiest thing was to call the team the 'Rest of the World', then I could also draft in Ken Doherty from Ireland and Tony Drago from Malta.

Once the selections were announced many argued that Cliff's World team was far stronger than Dennis' and would win comfortably. The fact it was generating debate amongst snooker fans was a good sign for me.

I've always admired how the Ryder Cup is able to get weeks of mileage and publicity out of what is really just a three-day event. The viewing figures on Sky for the opening ceremony itself usually compare well with coverage of a top Premier League football match; they are masters of exploiting their brand commercially. The clever thing that adds extra interest to the opening ceremony is that until that point the golfers do not know who they will be playing against. The captains announce their line-ups live on TV in front of a global audience. It's dramatic and I thought to myself, 'I'm nicking that.'

So before the first day's play we also decided to stage a launch dinner where the two captains would announce their pairings, and playing order. Not only that, a player from each side would play a match for the first point. This meant that as well as a dinner, and the speeches, the fans could see some snooker as well. It was limited to 150 people but it sold out really quickly just like the Higgins show in 2010. I'd undersold it!

Ticket sales up to the event itself were OK, but not spectacular. Then, of course just five days before the Legends Cup, Mr Ronnie O'Sullivan went and won the World Snooker Championship for the fourth time. That certainly helped.

Sadly, Ronnie was knackered after the championship and

didn't want to come to the dinner. I was a little upset but also worried how people would react. All the other players were there and there had already been Chinese whispers amongst fans about him not showing up for the weekend after his exploits in Sheffield. A few of the players had asked me, too. The guy had just won £250,000 for becoming world champion. Did he really want to roll up to Bedworth five days later for another weekend for a few grand, after being away from home for three weeks? Would you?

Worst of all, Ronnie wasn't the best at keeping in contact and would go silent for days, not answering his calls. I didn't have any reason to think he wouldn't show up but when everyone kept asking me over and over again, I'll admit now, the doubt crept in.

This was the biggest show we had ever done. Basically it was five of our normal shows over-packed into three days. I needed the Rocket.

The launch dinner went well. For snooker fans, having access to so many stars in one room was like being in a sweet shop. The soup and chicken supreme were passable – no one complained as far as I know. For the snooker at the dinner I'd asked Jimmy to represent England and Northern Ireland, and Tony Drago to play for the Rest for the World. I felt having captains Dennis and Cliff grind out a best of three could have seen us there till midnight!

Jimmy won a close match and Team England went 1-0 up. The captains made their speeches and announced their line-ups. Ronnie was first match on, partnering Dennis the next morning... but I had no idea where he was or if he was coming.

I went to my room about 11.30pm, just as the guys started a game of poker. While they were all having great fun and playing Texas Hold 'Em, I felt a headache coming on. It was undoubtedly 'Rocket fever'.

After not sleeping a great deal, I got the call at about 9am. 'Jase, it's Ronnie. I'll be with you in about two hours.'

It was a great relief but the minibus was leaving Weston Hall for the venue at 11. I bet my life he wouldn't be dressed ready to play.

Everyone was in high spirits and the friendly banter had started. Confirmation of Ronnie arriving just topped it off. Drago was sore at losing to Jimmy: Tony was the unofficial mascot for Cliff's team, full of high fives and hugs – I'm not sure what Stephen Hendry really made of it. As a man who had accomplished so much as an individual, in a largely individual sport, the idea of being part of a team wasn't something that initially came easy.

By 11am Drago had doubled up on breakfast and was into his second Mars Bar, adrenalin and a sugar high making for an explosive combination for the Tornado. Cliff was doing his Tony impression, and when they all clambered onto the bus, it was like the 'jolly boys outing' from a Christmas special of *Only Fools and Horses*. All we needed was a sing-song and a 'kiss me quick' hat, and of course for Del Boy not to blow up the bus with a dodgy radio imported from Moldova.

Ronnie arrived about ten past eleven. The bus had gone, and he had his dad with him. 'All right, Jase, traffic was a bit bad; can we get a bit of brekkie?'

Brekkie? I thought. We start the show in an hour and I need you down the venue.

'Full English, no mushrooms, mug of tea!' barked his dad, and the chef got to work.

It was nearer half past eleven before we left, but the two Ronnies, junior and senior, had enjoyed their grub and the mood seemed OK.

Ronnie's dad informed me he wanted a pass so he could go wherever he wanted to, and that he also had some guests turning up and wanted VIP tickets for them; they needed to be looked after. It felt a bit forceful, but I've learned that this is just his way. He only has one volume setting, and it tends to be on full most times.

I think Ronnie's dad was enjoying the chance to attend an event with his son. Because of what happened in the past, he doesn't show up at major tournaments. He probably feels it would be an unfair distraction for Ronnie and added pressure. We've always got on OK; we've had our moments, but he knows I always do what's best for his son, and that makes me all right by him.

England and Northern Ireland started well and led at the end of Day 1. To the delight of the crowd Ronnie had made a century.

In the players' room we showed the action as it happened on a big screen and Drago was bouncing off the walls, getting so involved. It was nice to see it meant so much to him, and his enthusiasm was infectious and spread to them all.

The score at the end of Day 1 was 9-4 in England and Northern Ireland's favour. Ronnie hadn't lost a game, Drago was angry at his team's performance and Jimmy was taking any opportunity to wind him up.

'What's the score, Tone?' said the Whirlwind.

'Did you win today?' was another dig.

Drago wasn't happy; it was a day for some serious comfort eating. Luckily in that department he couldn't be defeated.

We got the bus back to Weston Hall and the idea was we'd enjoy a Chinese meal and have a few drinks.

A few drinks.

Did I mention we'd have a few drinks?

I had a few drinks, Stephen had a few drinks, and Dennis had a few drinks... Ronnie... had a few drinks, then a few drinks more and then... well, the last thing I witnessed, as I went to bed at about 2am, was Ronnie sat with Hendry, telling him how much he loved him.

'You're the guv'nor you are, the best, the bollocks.'

Hendry was very patient about it, and it was quite amusing to see 11 world titles crammed into one armchair. Here was a man having a blow-out after 17 days of immense pressure in Sheffield. I didn't begrudge him that; I just wished he hadn't chosen to do it at my event.

Ronnie was chain-smoking, in the bar of a non-smoking hotel. 'It's OK, it's Ronnie,' they said. 'He can do whatever he likes.'

The irony of the similarities to how Alex Higgins once flouted authority and rules wasn't lost on Cliff Thorburn. 'Let's hope he doesn't shit in the wardrobe like Alex did once,' he said.

Fat chance of him even making it upstairs to his wardrobe, I thought to myself.

CHAPTER 23

THE LEGENDS CUP, YEAR ONE – DAY 2

At about 2am I extracted myself from the party and went to bed. It had been a long day, and part of me felt that by sleeping I didn't need to worry about what might be happening downstairs. I was physically and mentally exhausted. Surely, I thought, tomorrow will be less stressful?

I set my alarm and closed my eyes, desperate for rest. I glanced up at the smoke alarm above my bed. The little red flashing LED light was reassuring. At least I'd know soon enough if a stray roll-up set fire to the hotel.

When I got up at about 8am and went down to breakfast it was obvious that Ronnie wasn't going to be troubling the maid today. He was still up, his bed not slept in!

Ronnie and referee Jan Verhaas had done an all-nighter – quite impressive if you don't have to go and pot balls for a thousand people in a few hours. Remarkably, Jan seemed OK. They make them tough in the Netherlands, I thought; either that, or he was a bloody good actor.

Ronnie was still in his blue playing shirt. JV's daughter Brook-

Leah had stayed up too, but she had obviously stopped drinking many hours before and was trying to get him in some sort of order.

Everyone was stunned by the state of him.

'I can't play, Jase, I'm ruined.'

For once, words failed me.

I said to his mate, 'Scouse John', 'Get him in the shower quick. He's playing in two hours.'

John felt guilty; he'd been up as well. Ronnie's dad wasn't happy either; he knew it was unprofessional and blamed John.

Somehow we got Ronnie into a shower. I made sure it was cold! We dressed him and helped him onto the bus. I slapped some sunglasses on him and I just hoped we'd be able to get away with it because the crowds had gathered outside the stage door on Day 1.

'I'm only playing because it's you, Jase,' he slurred. 'Anyone else and I'd have stayed in bed today. Only cos it's you.'

I think I was meant to feel grateful. Maybe I was. Any sort of Ronnie was better than not having Ronnie at all. I kept telling myself it would be OK. The other guys were saying how sorry they felt for me. They were all running in the other direction from this situation though, wanting no part of it!

It was time to stick together. We collectively had to get this Rocket safely back on the ground, because trust me, at this particular time he was flying and way out of control. The England team was leading 9-4 but their prize asset was in another orbit.

SESSION 3, PART 1
England and NI: 9; Rest of the World: 4

The first match of the third session was doubles and it was Ronnie's turn to partner Jimmy – the partnership the fans had been waiting for, and one Dennis had been saving up to use. They were up against Stephen and Tony. Tony knew how important it was for Cliff to get off to a good start, trailing as they were, so he was probably the only one secretly delighted at the state the world champion was in.

First, before any play, we had the VIP reception – a chance for the people who had paid around £60 to sit in the best seats, meet all the players and have a glass of champagne.

On Day 1 at the previous two VIP receptions Ronnie had reluctantly walked in carrying the World Trophy. The crowd loved it, he didn't. He was also of course the last name announced and got the biggest cheer; he was our top of the bill.

Today, Ronnie could hardly stand, but when his name was called to enter the VIP room, he waddled in carrying the World Trophy between his legs like it was his... well, you can imagine.

Everyone laughed. 'It was just Ronnie being Ronnie.' I swear that weekend he could have walked on water. He was titanium.

JP said, 'I wonder what Joe Davis would have made of that.'

We all laughed and it broke the tension. We paraded him round the VIPs and then got him into his dressing room. Time was going to be the only cure for this hangover, but time was the one thing I didn't have.

We discussed moving his match to second on, but Jimmy quite rightly pointed out that if we got him through the doubles, he'd have a couple of hours to get his head down before a singles encounter. Ironically, that was against Stephen Hendry, the man whose lap he had been sitting on a few hours earlier.

People had been buzzing about their match-up from the night before when it was announced. Within the camp we assumed Stephen wouldn't have too much trouble against a misfiring Rocket!

I was relying on Jimmy, Stephen and Tony to get Ronnie through this. England won the toss and Ronnie decided to break. For some reason he decided to try a break-off shot where he would place the cue ball between green and brown, but hit it diagonally through the blue and pink to catch the reds on the opposite side. It's not even a break you would use in exhibitions.

Everyone could see he was still pissed; he slumped in the booth and leaned on Jimmy's shoulders, falling asleep at one point. I look back on it now and laugh – even Ronnie does – but at the time it was really stressful.

I was praying that either Stephen or Tony would get in quick and clear up. Cliff thought he was guaranteed a point. Ronnie had about two shots in the first frame; one a foul when he went for the blue instead of a red. There was an uneasy murmur in the audience; JV was doing his best not to draw attention to the fact Ronnie was very worse for wear.

Jimmy, being Jimmy, got in and made 70 and won the first frame on his own. ROS had a kip. Drago was mortified.

To everyone's amazement, halfway through the second frame, with the scores roughly level, Ronnie made the best drunk 48 break you will ever see: six reds and six blacks. Behind the scenes we were speechless; I think the three other players were too.

9-4 became 10-4 and England won the next doubles as well. It was turning into a rout. The score was 11-4 going into the third session singles.

The Rest of the World team were in trouble. To have any chance going into the final session they had to get three out of the four remaining points in the singles. The victory total was 18, and Dennis and co were already bearing down on it.

Fresh cakes arrived from the local bakery in the interval. Jimmy said, 'Better get one before Tony sees them', but the Tornado was nowhere to be seen and neither were any other members of his team.

Cliff had taken them off together for a little chat in the dressing room – a call to arms to basically pull their fingers out. Again, I think Stephen felt it was all getting a bit too serious.

SESSION 3, PART 2
England and NI: 11; Rest of the World: 4

Fate decided that first up in the singles was Ronnie v Stephen. A clash of the titans, a four-time world champion with the world's biggest hangover against a seven-time world champion with a Thorburn rallying speech ringing in his ears.

Stephen won and sparked a comeback. Tony, Cliff and Ken all won their singles. From 11-4 it was now 11-8. As a Liverpool football fan it felt a bit like Istanbul in 2005 when they came back from 3-0 down to win the Champions League. JV was pumping up the crowd. It was game on again with everything to play for going into the final session.

FINAL SESSION, PART 1
England and NI: 11; Rest of the World: 8

There were eight points on offer in this session, and Dennis needed seven of them or we were going to re-spots and sudden death. The draw came out. Dennis went with strength in the first half. Ronnie, Jimmy, JP, then himself. Cliff put Stephen on, then Tony, Ken, and left himself to face off with Dennis.

Ronnie was now feeling better and dominated Hendry to turn over the result from the afternoon's match. It became 12-8.

Jimmy followed on by beating Tony. It seemed as though the revival from the afternoon was over for the Rest of the World: now 13-8. But this wasn't over, and Ken and Cliff ground out victories to make it 13-10 going in to the final session.

FINAL SESSION, PART 2
England and NI: 13; Rest of the World: 10

Jimmy went out first to play Stephen; it was a Crucible rematch. Being three points behind, Cliff needed Hendry to pile more misery on Jimmy. Stephen responded, as champions do, and hit a 120 clearance. The break would go on to be the highest of the tournament.

Stephen had just made the last eight of the World Championship and hit a 147 maximum break on the way. He may have been retired but he was still sharp. There was no way he wanted to play second fiddle to anyone.

13-11, within two points again...

Next up: Ronnie v Drago. Tony had his chances, but I think if anything he was trying too hard and Ronnie nicked the frame: 14-11 now and within four points. JP took them a step closer beating Cliff, but then Ken turned Dennis over, so that at the end of normal play the score was 15-12. It was Sudden Death time.

SUDDEN DEATH – BLACK BALL RE-SPOTS
England and NI: 15; Rest of the World: 12

Each captain could nominate who would represent their team but they had to go through the entire team before anyone could shoot twice. Suddenly momentum swung and the first four black ball re-spots were all won by the Rest of the World.

Tony Drago was screaming. I feared he could have an aneurism, but the crowds loved it. The England and Northern Ireland team had gone quiet; JV was running out of superlatives. Remarkably the Rest of the World now led 16-15 and were just two points from victory.

Dennis went to the Whirlwind, to face Tony. It was tense. Four safety shots were exchanged before Jimmy was left with a half-chance. He nailed it, the crowd went wild, and even Ronnie was hugging him: 16-16.

Ronnie was up next. Everyone was smiling, but inside no one wanted to be the person who let the team down. Ken played a bad shot: adrenalin meant he over-hit the black by about four feet. Ronnie faced a tricky black across the nap... By now table etiquette had gone out of the window and there was banter flying from both teams. Ronnie held his nerve and potted it. England and Northern Ireland were once more in control at 17-16.

Fate almost decreed that with just one point needed for victory, and that victory possible with the potting of a final black ball, Captain Dennis Taylor would step up for his team. Cliff had to win this point or the fight back would have been in vain.

Cliff played a dump shot to the side cushion; Dennis had a double on, a 'Barney Rubble' as we call it. Would he go for it? Of course he would. For once there was no time for a gag, no telling any stories about his brother Seamus (he never had a brother called Seamus, by the way). This was tense.

Standing where he was, Dennis knew the ball was in before anyone else. His team went mad. England and Northern Ireland had won the Legends Cup!

JP performed his own 'Dennis 1985' finger wag and everyone embraced. Ken, Stephen and Cliff smiled and congratulated the team, and so did Tony, but the Tornado was hurting.

Victory speeches were made, confetti fired, and although one team had beaten the other, everyone had played their part in putting on a fantastic event. As Ronnie left, still not trusted to drive, he said to me, 'You're a clever c**t with them black-ball finishes, Jase.'

It's not a quote I can often repeat out loud, and people say the funniest of things when they are drunk, but it meant a lot.

CHAPTER 24

THE 2012 TOUR

Two thousand and twelve was a pivotal year for Snooker Legends. As well as the first staging of the Legends Cup, we also played shows in Ireland, Jersey, Preston, Radlett, Stoke, Telford and Ipswich. We also played a show at the Fairfield Halls in Croydon. It was a 'Ronnie night' and the Rocket was firing on all cylinders, making our tour's third maximum 147 break.

Eighteen centuries were made in total that year, again not a bad return over 12 shows. We were now an established part of the Snooker Show fraternity, building a reputation for good shows with access to the players. Sales-wise the wage bill was going up with Ronnie on the bill, but so were the ticket numbers. Not every show was making money, but as long as a few more were making more than the others lost it was OK and we building, still aiming for our product to be recognised as being viable for TV.

However, I felt a bit like Alex Ferguson: I had to break up the original winning team. It was hard to do emotionally but I knew it was a correct commercial decision. I'd based the first two years largely on the same four players, but with the addition of

Hendry, Davis and O'Sullivan I was now spoilt for choice, and the casualties from regular shows became JP and Cliff.

JP also lost his horse-racing contract with the BBC at the same time, as the sport's coverage moved to Channel 4, so it was a double blow for him. I'm sure John wasn't reliant on the Legends for income but I know how much he enjoyed them. For a while he only did a few shows, but my new World Seniors Tour put him right back in the mix. He loves the golf days too.

With Cliff it was more a financial decision, as return flights from Toronto aren't cheap, plus of course he has to have accommodation during all the downtime between shows. At the time of writing, I am desperately trying to take the Seniors Tour to Canada where he can be the headline act. Twice we've been close to finding sponsors to fund it and twice it's fallen through. I do feel for him, as I know how much he loves being involved in the game.

It's fair to say in 2012 my first-choice line-up for a four-man show was now Jimmy, Dennis, Steve Davis and Stephen Hendry. Within a few shows of putting them together, Stephen and Steve formed this new double act. It was like Peter Kay and Victor Meldrew – Davis was Kay! Steve is without doubt, as I have mentioned before, the best exhibition player I have ever seen, and Stephen has a naturally dry sense of humour. They dovetail so well. In the other pairing it's much simpler: Jimmy pots the balls and Dennis tells the gags. With JV and Michaela, the team is a tried and tested formula.

I never put Ronnie in a four-man line-up. I did it once in Berlin and it didn't work. No disrespect to the other players, but if you put him on the bill, then people want to see him playing all the time, not sat in the dressing room while others play.

Generally on a two-man show it's Ronnie and Jimmy, although in 2016 I did an Eleven Thirty series with Judd and have also taken Mark Selby to Germany, Romania and Bulgaria. Sometimes I will use Stephen and Jimmy: their Crucible history

Left and above: Jimmy White's testimonial – The plan for Ronnie Wood strumming guitar on a bar stool turned into a £20,000 Rolling Stones reunion with Mick Hucknall guest vocalist.

Below: Auctioneer Willie Thorne with a 'Spin Cue' painted by Damien Hirst.

Left: I did the deal with JK from Rok Stars to facilitate Ronnie's return to Snooker in 2013.

Right: Another Team Ronnie Masters Victory.

Left: Getting a spin in Ronnie's Ferrari.

Right: It ended pretty well and it was nice to get acknowledged on the lap of honour.

5.30pm   Snooker: Legends Cup   DS,W
Day one of the Legends Cup at the Civic Hall in Bedworth,
featuring Ronnie O'Sullivan, Dennis Taylor, Steve Davis, Stephen
Hendry, Jimmy White, Cliff Thurburn and Neil Robertson.

Press ⓘ for more   6.45pm Su 05/05

Sports	News	Kids	Music	Shop	Religion	Internat'l	Gaming

- - -	Saturday	6.30pm	7.00pm	7.30pm	ch+
409 Sky Sports 3	Live YB40 Cricket			Osasuna v Getafe-L..
410 Eurosport HD	WTA Tennis			
411 Eurosport 2 HD	◀ Ⓡ Snooker: Legends Cup			ⓇLive Snooker: Le..
412 Eurosport	WTA Tennis			
413 MOTORS TV UK	NASCAR Nationwide Series			
415 At The Races	Stateside			
417 ESPN HD	Live: Manchester City v Wigan -...			
418 MUTV	My Mate: Manchest..	United 360		The United Archive..

⦿ On Demand   ⦿ Planner   ⦿ +24 Hours   ⦿ -24 Hours   ch-

The 2013 Rok Stars Legends Cup.

Filming with Tony Drago in Malta. The documentary is one of my proudest pieces of work. It was warts and all, fair to say the Tornado wasn't a fan of flying.

Snooker in Goffs, Co Kildare is pretty special…

Above: The King of the Crucible.

Below: Ronnie wore my logo in the 2014 World Champs.

Above left: Jimmy White 2017 UK Seniors Champion.

Above right: Cliff Thorburn 2018 Senior Masters Champion.

Below: Steve Davis 2018 Irish Seniors Masters Champion. Steve was presented with the iconic trophy by Lauren Higgins, Daughter of The Hurricane.

Above left: The 2018 Assetereum World Seniors Snooker Champion Aaron Canavan from Jersey. He Dared to Dream.

Above right: My Last tournament with Ronnie, the 2017 UK Champs… went ok didn't it?

Below left: Mrs Snooker Legends, supports every crazy idea I have.

Below right: Dennis Taylor.

makes it a good story to base the night on and I bill the match-ups as 'Crucible Memories'. In 2015 it was 25 years since Stephen first won his first World Championship, and I was planning some nights to commemorate that. I pulled them when it was clear they wouldn't sell.

It seemed as if the current World Snooker contracts were going to prevent Jimmy playing in our World Seniors shows, but my recent collaboration with the WPBSA has paved the way to allow all invitational wildcards to participate. That's common sense; that's commercial value for my future plans...

CHAPTER 25

DECISIONS AND REVELATIONS

14th February 2013: 11:30pm

The call came in from Los Angeles...

'I think we should do it; I've spoken to my partner and we've allocated a million dollars to make this happen.'

JUNE 2013

My mouse hovered over the email. I knew if I opened it that I was no better than them, but if I didn't, then I was denying myself the proof of knowing what I had been suspecting for some time.

It wasn't the first time I'd been copied into an email by mistake. After all, my name being Jason Francis, and the chairman of the World Professional Billiards and Snooker Association (WPBSA) being Jason Ferguson, the margin for error was always there, especially as many email programs now autosuggest the recipient after you've only typed the first letter. It's amazing the amount of sensitive information that has dropped into my inbox over the past few years!

The disappointing thing about what I suspected the content of this email would be was that I truly thought we'd got past this issue. Barry Hearn had reiterated to me on numerous occasions, both in person and via email, that he was fully supportive of the Legends Tour. In some respects I was doing a job for him by providing an income and employment for some of the retired players – players really that previous World Snooker hierarchy had dumped like over-aged racehorses who aren't good for anything more than the knacker's yard.

There are some good people within World Snooker. Jason Ferguson is a beacon of common sense and fairness, and someone who has helped tremendously in making the World Seniors project happen. I also have to say I've found the staff in Bristol incredibly efficient and friendly – then again, what I was doing in Legends in 2013 wasn't in any way directly affecting their jobs, and I would hope I am always courteous and polite in all my dealings with them. Sadly at that time, some people at the very highest echelons of World Snooker were developing issues with me and my Legends Tour. Why? Well...

If, for example, you are a commercial director, and spend most of your time in China apologising and explaining why the game's most marketable commodity hasn't travelled again to your tournaments, which in 2013 Ronnie didn't... and then you see plans for him to appear in China at a Snooker Legends event, I can understand you being a bit annoyed.

Also if, for example, you are a salaried director of World Snooker Ltd at that time, but you also manage one of the top eight players in the game and are co-promoter for all WSL German events, I guess the sight of the world champion playing in Berlin for Snooker Legends and not in the German Masters may not sit right...

I don't blame Barry Hearn; he makes no apologies for who he

is and what he does. Surprisingly, I almost respect him for that – not that he is relying on my respect or anyone else's to make his day worthwhile. Barry is Barry, a far more successful promoter than I will ever be, and a far more ruthless man than I could ever want to be. He also knows what it's like to put his hand in his pocket and risk his own money. Ask any promoter how often they get everything right; we make money, we lose money, you just gotta hope you make more than you lose!

I didn't expect everyone to be happy with the growth or success of Legends – that's business – but I knew the 'double click' was going to end up opening much more than a bitter email.

Snooker Legends had just achieved 12.3 million viewers on Eurosport, an event World Snooker sanctioned and supported, and Legends was now going to Berlin with Ronnie, the current world champion, heading the bill.

The content of the email was around a plan to, and I quote, 'kick out the Snooker Legends' and damage the relationship I had started with Eurosport.

Photos after the event of empty seats in the 2,500-seater Berlin Tempodrom were circulated with captions like 'Spot the crowd'. Barry wasn't involved; he's a promoter, and I'd like to believe no decent promoter, no matter how competitive you may be, should enjoy seeing another one lose their shirt.

Everyone, including Ronnie, told me to cancel the show, to give in, to save myself 20,000 euros, but no way was I going to be bullied. It didn't matter to me if I lost 100,000 euros. Looking back I should thank them for teaching me another big lesson.

You can't put a price on loyalty and friendship, or your integrity. I did the event, kept quiet, but made sure everyone in our team saw exactly what had happened. And you know what? Sometimes if the bully upsets the apple cart, so to speak, he may find the next time he wants to buy those apples, the price goes up!

I can't imagine there was a time Ronnie, Jimmy White,

Michaela Tabb or Stephen Hendry all travelled abroad on a three-day playing trip and collectively refused to be paid for a show they played in – that's what being part of a team is.

The second, almost larger irony is that if I'd taken a different course following that phone call quoted at the start of this chapter from Los Angeles in February, the announcement after my Legends Cup wouldn't have been about a one-night exhibition in Germany: it would have been about splitting the world of snooker in two.

Long before that, I'd become increasingly frustrated by the contract restrictions on players by World Snooker that scuppered plans to stage events with BTV6 and CCTV in China, featuring, of course, Ronnie O'Sullivan. At a meeting at Alexandra Palace at the 2013 Masters tournament, I was invited to the board meeting and asked them why they wouldn't allow this. I had previously requested many times to try to find a way to work together, to integrate the Legends Tour. I'd proved beyond doubt we had an audience for it and snooker fans enjoyed the nights. I wasn't to know at that point it would take me another five years to get a partnership in place with the governing body.

The commercial director said that it wouldn't be in his interests to allow it to proceed – which in layman's terms meant 'If you turn up in China with Ronnie you will damage our business'!

Barry wasn't at the meeting but his number two, Steve Dawson, was, and so was Jason Ferguson, although, from what I could see, he couldn't really impact what happened on the World Snooker board as he headed up the WPBSA, the governing body and custodian of the sport. Steve chaired the meeting, and the commercial director made sure I didn't get my China sanction *but* I got assurances that if I met all the sanction criteria, then any reasonable request for a future sanction wouldn't be refused.

Later that day the commercial director received a call from the acquisitions manager at Eurosport responsible for snooker, explaining that they would like to televise my Legends Cup the weekend after the 2013 World Championship. I guess it was just coincidence!

With no clashing tournaments, and the leverage a direct request from their major European broadcast partner brought in, they had no option but to approve it. Had they not, then perhaps I would have revisited the conversations of February 14th Valentine's night, a night I was falling out of love with snooker whilst couples were proclaiming theirs to each other.

I had the chance to split the sport in two; it was as simple as that. The implementation of the Professional Snooker Players Federation (PSPF) would have done to World Snooker what Barry Hearn and his PDC Darts Organisation did to the British Darts Organisation (BDO).

By October 2012, Ronnie was interested. He had effectively retired: he'd not played properly since the World Championship in May and had just pulled out of the 2012 International Open, the story I told earlier. We were in the middle of a six-date tour of the UK and, day by day, the vision of forming our own world snooker tour was becoming more of a viable proposition.

Jimmy White and Michaela Tabb were ready to jump ship if the money was right. Jimmy was hardly earning from the tour any more. More importantly, I had verbally secured the funding to guarantee eight global events in year one with eight professionals guaranteed £150,000 a year basic salary before any additional tournament or commercial earnings. As well as the players who were party to these confidential discussions, we had targeted Neil Robertson (Australia), Ding Junhui (China), John Higgins, Stephen Hendry (Scotland) and Alex Pagulayan. Alex would bring us Canada and was known in the USA. Four local, relevant wildcards would be chosen for each event, and we had targeted tournaments in London, Ireland, Malta, Sydney, Shanghai, Vegas and Berlin, with the World Championship in the UK in year one but then moving to the home of whoever had won it for year two – thus maximising the commercial power of the defending world champion bringing the championship home to his country.

We were going to fund all travel and accommodation; events were four to seven days long, world champs longer; and there would be different formats for different events – so, for example, some with random draws each round, the now infamous Legends black ball re-spots for deciding frames for others, etc. The idea was also that the players would be commentating when not playing, to give them a new skill and some media training and experience.

The main thing we had to offer was that the eight players we eventually chose would become shareholders in the PSPF parent company and organisation. What they brought into the organisation as players then, would continue to give them a revenue stream long after they had retired. I'd like to think it was quite forward thinking.

We had everything we needed, including now, of course, the promise of funding, but it was clear to me we'd need to be sustainable as a business after year one, and of course I'd be single-handedly responsible for ripping apart the sport I loved. I was fighting with the fact that it was some of the people who were running the sport that were my problem, not the sport itself.

I was also asking Ronnie, Jimmy and others to turn their back on their association, something, almost ironically, Barry and the darts players did in the blink of an eye in 1992. I just couldn't do it, although believe me it came closer than anyone ever knew at some points. I was being driven by frustration and ambition and not by a yet sustainable business plan.

We'd even provisionally booked a Legends event in Goffs in Ireland, under the ruse of an invitational tournament, to get the 16 players we wanted into the Citywest Hotel to discuss the proposal and get secrecy agreements signed. It was exciting and torturous at the same time. I knew once these players committed, they would never be allowed back into Barry's club, and I had serious concerns about the retributions and taking him on. Barry hasn't got where he is today without ruffling a few feathers; he's forgotten more about the sport than I will ever know about it, although the irony isn't lost on me that for many years the sport he now owns regarded him as their biggest nemesis.

We both gave evidence at a court case for Jimmy White where he was accused of betting on his matches. It wasn't lost on me that while we were waiting in the corridor of chambers Barry was able to recount a number of memorable battles he had participated in against people who had tried to dethrone him or threaten his business.

Not one of the players we talked to worried about the sustainability of a new tour. I think the guaranteed salary probably turned their heads.

At the end of the day I decided I wanted to be known as the guy who created the Legends Tour, not the bloke who tried to split snooker in two and rob it of its most prized assets, just because a couple of people within World Snooker annoyed him. I hope with my recent collaboration I will value the decision I made back then.

CHAPTER 26

THE YEAR 2013 AND THE DEAL WITH EUROSPORT

At the start of 2013 the only place you could see Ronnie O'Sullivan play snooker was on the Legends Tour. Looking back, it was a position I could have exploited more than I did. Perhaps it was commercial madness to get him the ROK deal to return to snooker, but I always felt playing a major part in that would pay me back further down the line.

We travelled to Goffs in Ireland in February and I staged Ronnie and Steve Davis. I also took Dennis in the commentary role instead of JV.

Not having Jimmy around was weird to start with, but to also not have the reassuring presence of JV made it feel like a different show. However, I was still aware that we needed to keep evolving, and JV and Jimmy had played three shows there already. With the exception of the Rocket, audience numbers will naturally drop the second time you return to the same venue unless you freshen the line-up.

With Ronnie on the bill it sold out, of course, and he played beautifully while fending off the numerous questions about him returning for the World Championship.

For a few months, up to Sheffield, my own tour took a backseat to the 'assistant manager's' role I was playing for him. It had been announced that he was due, and contracted, to play in my Legends show in Sheffield that April, but once world snooker realised the implications of me having the World Champion in the Crucible when they couldn't get him I had Barry on the phone.

This time I was in a position of strength and I had to ask myself what Barry would have done if the roles had been reversed. In a game of poker I had the winning hand; how much was I prepared to bluff it up?

The issue was I knew Ronnie *was* going to enter the World Championship, but the deal with ROK included an embargo on disclosing it. Once that did come out then Ronnie would have to sign the player's contract which would have meant appearing for me in Sheffield at the same time as the qualifying was on for the main championship, and would have put him in breach.

Throughout the call I tried to hint as best I could the reason why I agreed to replace Ronnie in return for permission to use Davis and Jimmy. I truly think Barry just thought I was being helpful, which I guess I was in some respects.

I was averting a huge PR disaster for World Snooker, but also I'd been staging this particular show for years. The conflict with all professional snooker player's contracts occurred when they started trying to commercialise and charge spectators for the qualifiers at the English Institute of Sport down the road.

What I had done during this time was punt my product out to all the major broadcasters. Without Ronnie, their ratings were dropping: Sky had already decided they were going to cut right back on snooker.

All the major broadcasters responded, except Sky, and I got meetings with BT Sport and ITV. Every time, though, the same thing came up: they either already had existing contracts with Matchroom Sport, Barry's company, or an existing relationship with Barry himself that they valued.

The only other snooker aside from Barry to date had been something called Power Snooker, a form of snooker that was notable for two things:

1. People couldn't understand the rules, even the referees!
2. It became acceptable, in fact encouraged, to shout out to players, resulting in particularly harsh personal abuse of Shaun Murphy.

Ronnie had been paid a lot of money to front it. The guys behind the project were good theatre producers and they'd got some money via boxing promoter Frank Warren. The ballpark figure banded about was that they lost about £250,000 on the first show at the O2, and then they staged it in Manchester and lost a similar amount.

Throw as much money as you like at something, but if the issue is that the fans and players don't like it, how will it ever grow? Why didn't it work? Well who am I to say or criticise, but the cloth they chose to play it on was so fast it could make the players look silly, and you did need a degree in maths to keep up to date with the scoring. Double points for this, triple points in a power play, ball in hand... Quite frankly, it was messy.

I know they are still trying to resurrect the idea of Power Snooker, this time building it around an IPO for a crypto currency. How do I know this? Well they've asked to secure my services to develop the events for them. Our first show is due in 2019 so we will see, maybe with more simplified rules and my idea of a 'winner takes all' prize it could catch the imagination.

Out of the blue, late 2012, I got a call from Eurosport. Behind the scenes, and unbeknown to me, they had been contemplating trying my events for some time – no doubt the Ronnie ratings factor again. The Legends Cup gave them something different and guaranteed them the big names.

There were a number of issues, namely getting the World Snooker sanction I referred to earlier, but also, as I had an unproven product, I had to commit to raising an awful lot of money towards the production costs.

I took a punt and said I could do it. The wheels were set in motion. I didn't have a sponsor, but when Eurosport started putting pressure on World Snooker to grant my sanction then suddenly I became viable.

I was moving from staging nice little exhibitions in theatres in the UK to a global TV audience that could in theory cannibalise theirs. I understood the risks, but I was a big boy and I felt that getting a TV broadcast had to be the next step for the brand.

Having just helped secure the sponsorship deal for Ronnie to return to the sport, ROK, the 'Oval vodka' company, as I called them, seemed an obvious choice to approach as a partner. I laid out a full presentation to JK and his team, and explained we could brand the event not only with his vodka but with his beer company too. The potential reach for Eurosport was huge but French law meant that we couldn't call the event after one of the alcoholic brands. JK's parent company was called ROK Stars and so the ROK Stars Legends Cup was created, with one team wearing the Oval Vodka logos and the other wearing the ABK Bavarian Beer logos.

The company couldn't pay up front though. It was a risk and maybe not one I would have taken had my personal circumstances not recently changed. I had had responsibilities but now I didn't. I had been living with my partner and her four children in a large house in Essex. When the Legends Tour began, it was never my intention to tour with every show. I hadn't been 'on the road', so to speak, for ten years as a touring actor, and realistically being away from home so much wasn't part of the plan.

After Sheffield and Higgins it became clear to all that I had to be at every show. This wasn't something that could run itself or be trusted to an assistant. The strain of doing 50 away trips in two years took a toll on my personal life and the relationship broke down. I moved into rented accommodation and really shed myself of all my commitments and responsibilities; it was because of this that I was able to take a gamble with this production. I only had myself to worry about.

All of a sudden it became very real. I had my sanction. I had my broadcast. Snooker Legends was going to be live with a potential reach of 132 million people in 32 countries. I took a moment to thank Peter Ebdon and Graeme Dott, as I explained earlier they were responsible for giving me the idea of Snooker Legends in the first place.

However running a normal event and running a live TV event were two completely different things. Added to that, the nature of our event meant that players were changing over after each frame, a logistical nightmare when you literally have the commercial break to get it sorted.

We did venue visits and decided we'd go back to Bedworth. I felt good about that; they'd finally got a chance to put the venue on the map. Live TV was coming. Tickets were slow: was it punters' lethargy after seeing the event last year, or did the fact you could sit at home and watch this event from the comfort of your armchair mean people didn't want to attend in person? I know from being a football fan that nowadays I'd rather watch the action at home on Sky than pay high ticket prices to sit in the cold at the ground, staring at ants running around half a mile away. Its hard to sell tickets nowadays, we've made all live performances too easy to access on any platform you want.

For the second year of the Legends Cup the line-up was almost the same as year one, with just one change to each team. Steve

Davis was going to play for England and Northern Ireland, and Neil Robertson was going to join the Rest of the World.

JP and Ken were the two players who got replaced. I felt bad and a bit disloyal, but getting Steve Davis, a six-times world champion, to play was a no-brainer, and Neil was from Australia, world ranked number one, and of course the 2010 world champion.

Ronnie did his trick again, won the World's, and this time he attended our launch dinner! I'm not sure how much the fact that the event sponsor was also his tour sponsor had to do with it, but everyone was glad he was there. However, this time I couldn't get in contact with Neil; if it wasn't one thing it was another.

I'd only met Neil briefly once when we were at the Masters promoting Jimmy's testimonial. He seemed OK and we worked direct. He had a reputation for being pretty disorganised; he was late to a couple of Premier League matches and obviously needed a proper manager.

About a month before the event I met a guy called Mukesh at the World's. Muke, as he was known, had been Mark Selby's manager for a few years and had done very well out of it. Then I think Mark met Vikki, Muke met his wife to be, and things got a bit complicated. They split just before the World's and Muke said he'd started managing Neil.

OK, I thought, it kind of made sense, but I immediately got the impression that any agreement they had made had somehow got lost in translation. I truly believe Muke thought he was managing Neil, but I don't think Neil thought it was an official arrangement.

Anyway, I got a call from Muke just before the event asking for tickets for the launch dinner. No problem, as Neil's manager it's a courtesy I was happy to extend. However, it all became a bit farcical when Neil went AWOL on the day and his new 'manager' obviously didn't have a clue where he was or what he was up to. I was pretty fed up. I had the pressure of Eurosport,

I was entertaining my sponsors, but once again a top player was missing. I felt that, instead of enjoying my hospitality at the launch dinner, Muke should have been in his car down the A14, tracking down his client and dragging his arse to Bedworth as he was contracted to be at the event.

Neil had perforated his eardrum, so there was a legitimate excuse, but his communication was poor, and initially it didn't give me a good impression of him. Fortunately when he did arrive the next morning he was a dream all weekend, and he's someone I like and always chat to at events. He's got himself a competent proven manager now, but sadly that management has priced him out of working at current Legends events. I hope that changes in time as he is a hell of a player and one of the few who can stand toe-to-toe with Ronnie.

We got the news that the first afternoon would be a delayed broadcast, with us going live in the evening. That did give us a chance to ease ourselves into the event. I was going to act as tournament director, which meant wearing a headset and being in constant communication with the broadcast director. I blagged that it was fine. I may have seemed in control but I was nervous. Sometimes running a Legends show is more about managing what's going on away from the table than simply on it.

Ronnie wasn't a fan of us having TV at our events; he feels it takes the fun out of it. I do know what he means and, having done it, accept having the brand on TV isn't the be-all and end-all, but it does give you huge global exposure for your product.

At the launch dinner it was Jimmy and Tony who faced off for the second year running. The result was the same, and Team England and Northern Ireland went into Day 1 leading by one point. I took to my bed at Weston Hall knowing that although the Rocket was safely tucked up, we were about to go global. What on earth had I created...?

CHAPTER 27

EUROSPORT LEGENDS CUP, 12.3M

DAY 1, SESSION 1

England and NI: 1; Rest of the World: 0

Going into Day 1 Cliff was very aware that he couldn't let his opponents get a good start like they had the year before. He knew that Dennis liked to load his draw top-heavy, but in Neil Robertson he felt he had someone who could take Ronnie on, and try to neutralise his scoring power.

The first match-up of doubles saw Dennis and Ronnie beat Stephen and Neil, but then Cliff and a real in-form Tony turned over Jimmy and Steve. Honours even.

Even at this stage I had a feeling the matches were going to be very even. The event was coming across well to the TV guys, with plenty of humour. The biggest compliment I could pay JV is that Eurosport decided to mute all their own commentators while the frames were on and simply let JV run the show. They only top and tailed, and took us in and out of commercial breaks. I think it was being translated into five or six languages.

Going into the singles we were still waiting for our first century. Ronnie played beautifully to make 78 and beat Stephen, but Neil hit straight back for Cliff and beat Steve, blow for blow. Jimmy was in with 106 against Cliff, then Drago muscled Dennis out of a frame and celebrated like he had already won the Cup. The first session ended at three each, with only the point from the night before giving Dennis a slight advantage.

The players were also playing for two individual prizes: the £1,000 high break as normal, but also a newly created 'MVP', most valuable player. Again it was something I had unashamedly stolen from the NFL in America, but it was another responsibility I bestowed on JV.

The prize wasn't bad either: a Swarovski crystal-clad bottle of Oval vodka, estimated to be worth £5,000. It was worth winning, and of course it was full of premium-structured vodka.

We went back to the hotel for a break, just in time to see the afternoon's play broadcast on TV. It was a great moment and I shared it with my mate, Michaela. She had been there from the very start, the very first show.

My phone started bleeping. People were watching, comments were nice. I felt good. It all seemed worthwhile.

Back on the bus, and session two was ready to break off.

DAY 1, SESSION 2
England and NI: 4; Rest of the World: 3

As this event was a bit different, Eurosport were encouraging JV to have chats with the players in the arena. They then decided they'd like to do some interviews in the players' room – see how the players were feeling, and get their views on the match. Nowadays you see Eurosport on-site in their own studio, a relaxed sofa and interviews round the table; this type of thing had never been done before our Legends Cup.

I was the only one who could do those interviews, and in truth I think they knew the best chance they had of getting Ronnie on camera was if I asked him. The interview I did with him also included Michaela. Here they were having a laugh and a joke with each other, but only five or six days earlier, Michaela had to discipline Ronnie for a 'cue masturbation' gesture he made in his semi-final match with Judd at the World's. It was pretty serious at the time, and on reflection Michaela was right to do it, even though Ronnie claimed he was cleaning his cue. But no grudges were held on either side; here they were making each other tea and chatting like the best of mates.

Cliff put Hendry and Drago out in the first doubles; they were up against Ronnie and Steve. Of all the players, Ronnie looks up to Steve Davis. While many kids were Alex Higgins or Jimmy White fans, for Ronnie there was only one guv'nor: the Nugget. Ronnie still has a picture of him getting Steve's signature when he was 11 years old.

Drago dominated the first frame. His fist was pumping and he was exuberant, but this match was a best of three. Much as Drago tried to get Hendry involved in the emotion of it, Stephen really found it tough to let go. He'd hardly smiled when he won his world titles; he was hardly going to cry like Gazza at an exhibition.

Frame 2 and Drago went in with 52, in under 2 minutes. He was literally running round the table. It was very entertaining but, as so often happened in Tony's career, he missed a simple ball and let Ronnie in. Ronnie cleared beautifully with 65 and then potted the re-spotted black; it was first blood to Dennis again. Tony looked devastated; the mood back in the players' room wasn't great. I ordered the girls to restock the chocolate bowl!

Cliff and Neil hit straight back for the Rest of the World but again it took a great 63 from Robertson to nick it; the doubles were shared.

Ronnie won the first singles against Neil, but Stephen hit back with a break of 111. His opponent on the end of the drubbing was, of course, Jimmy. Tony beat Dennis, and then Steve beat Cliff, so overnight it was 7-6.

'Let's have some Chinese,' Ronnie said. The colour must have drained from my face as I was transported back 12 months.

He laughed. 'Don't worry, Jase, I ain't drinking tonight. Wanna do a run in the morning.'

Ronnie did drink but it was the odd glass of wine, and he was in bed before me. Feedback had come in from Eurosport: it was going well.

However, the Legends event girls were starting to get some social-media abuse. They'd been used as walk-on girls and had been part of the team for years, known to all of the players. Photos had appeared of them with the guys before, but now it seemed some fans were jealous. Both Georgie and Michelle posted pictures of themselves with Ronnie and Stephen, and 'slut', 'slag', 'whore' were all words that followed. It was unacceptable, and another downside to getting the brand on TV.

DAY 2, SESSION 3

England and NI: 7; Rest of the World: 6

Jimmy and a perfectly sober Ronnie went out first and battered Tony and Neil. Ronnie made 117; it would be the highest break of the tournament. The same tit-for-tat continued with neither team able to break away.

By the end of session three, the scores were 10-9, the only highlight of the singles being a hundred from Hendry, his second of the tournament.

DAY 2, SESSION 4

England and NI: 10; Rest of the World: 9

Both teams needed to get to 18; Rest of the World had never led, but had never trailed by more than one point either. The all-important singles were upon us.

I'm not sure what Cliff said, but suddenly they caught fire. They won the first four singles matches. Neil beat Ronnie, his first defeat of the tournament; an inspired Tony beat Jimmy; Stephen beat Steve; and Cliff grinded Dennis. Suddenly it was 13-10 and Cliff could sniff victory.

Dennis went to Jimmy to stop the rot; it didn't work. Robertson was flying and a 90 made it 14-10. Relief came as the Rocket defeated Hendry, and Dennis was inspired and defeated Tony. With one singles match to go it was 14-12. It was a repeat of the 1983 World Final: the Nugget Steve Davis against the Grinder Cliff Thorburn.

It was no secret that in their playing days these two didn't get on. It would be easy to say it was all Steve, but I don't think Cliff ever thought he consistently got the better of Steve, which can make you grumpy. In this frame Cliff lived up to his catchphrase: 'every shot was a pint of blood'. He won and took his team to within three points at 15-12.

SUDDEN DEATH – BLACK BALL RE-SPOTS

England and NI: 12; Rest of the World: 15

Just 12 months earlier the scores had been reversed. Dennis still had a chance. First up were Drago and Jimmy. Drago nailed it for 16-12 and celebrated like it was over. Even his team mates laughed at his reaction. It was electric in the arena, and I could only hope that it was translating that way on the screen at home.

Cliff was up next against Steve, and the Nugget played a good up-and-down shot leaving the black only a few inches off the top cushion. Cliff eyed up the cut. Surely he had to play safe? If anyone would play safe it would be Cliff, wouldn't it?

Not a chance. Cliff cut the black in; Robertson jumped up at the same time as Drago and almost knocked Tony out with the butt of his cue. No one noticed until Tony sat covering his eye. It was chaos. The Rest of the World were within one point of taking the Legends Cup. Dennis turned to Ronnie.

Ronnie played a great shot, Neil replied, they went back and forth. Ronnie knowing that he couldn't afford to leave Neil a half-chance. Ronnie caught a safety too thick and the ball headed diagonally down the table. It seemed as if everything went into slow motion as it headed for the pocket. In truth this wasn't how I wanted it to end: in any penalty shoot-out you want the winner to be scored, not a victory gifted by the opponent missing.

Neil theatrically pretended to blow the ball towards the pocket. There was no need: the cloth was so fast the ending was inevitable. The cue ball dropped in, the Cup was won, Drago was bouncing, and Ronnie genuinely looked gutted.

Cliff took the trophy and made a speech that will stay with me forever. Here was a man who had won everything the game had to offer, and in the midst of a victory in a team exhibition he stopped to pay tribute to me live on TV: 'Jason, mate, we did it. God bless you, man.'

The cameras did a close-up on me, looking like a cock in my headset. I looked knackered, and the camera didn't lie, although of course it did add ten pounds, right?

The MVP was won by Tony. He promptly took the £5,000 bottle of vodka and emptied it down the toilet. 'I don't drink,' he said.

Jimmy shook his head in disbelief. Yes, the value was in the bottle, but £100 of premium vodka had been thrown away – but that's Tony.

It was an amazing event. The theatricals and nature of Drago got me thinking about another idea. I wanted to make a fly-on-the-wall documentary about him. Even that night in the bar, when I should have been enjoying a beer, my mind was already on to my next project – and it was going to involve a little trip to Malta.

CHAPTER 28

DRAGO

In 2014 I spent a few months planning, filming and editing the Tony Drago documentary. I was interviewed about the project before it started and I was asked to describe him to anyone who didn't know who he was.

I said…

'Tony Drago is a 49-year-old cue sports legend from Malta. He's passionate, impatient, lightning fast and [long pause] usually hungry…'

It was an off-the-cuff remark and the reporter laughed but it actually ended up as the opening narrative of the finished piece and, on reflection, it did sum him up at that time. It wasn't meant as derogatory, quite the opposite in fact.

It was going to be a small TV production set-up of myself, Drago and a cameraman called Stewart. From the off I knew it was going to test my patience.

Stewart headed up ROK TV at the time, so it was all done in-house. Tony has a heart of gold but he has a short temper and can be obnoxious and rude. If you don't know him you can take offence easily; part of this is what makes him great value to watch playing snooker but not the best to work with, especially when you ask him to be part of a team. Stewart was very well educated, Oxford or Cambridge I think, and spoke very well. He sounded proper posh! I felt a little bit in the middle from day one, acting as director, producer and United Nations peacemaker. There hadn't been any notable disagreements between Malta and the United Kingdom since the island got its independence in 1964. I was keen not to manufacture the first.

We did our first filming at a Players Tour Championship (PTC) event in Doncaster. World Snooker granted us access and we spent a few hours interviewing Tony and following him about while he played his first round. I was surprised at how passionately he spoke about his career. Here was a kid from Malta, who had left home at 18 to come and live in England to play snooker. Straight away he was homesick; he remained so until he fell off-tour in 2016 and returned full-time to the archipelago.

The idea was we would do a couple of days in Doncaster but then we'd all go to Malta and film him there to find out how his snooker career first began. We titled the project from one of Tony's quotes when describing himself: 'Fun and torture at the same time'. I loved it.

Tony was good value and I knew how to press the right buttons so we could get the full range of emotions: anger at being ripped-off by a manager when he was young, tears when he talked about his mother, and frustration when your scampi and chips turn up 30 seconds before his! Take some time to google his post-match reaction against Alan McManus at the German Masters Qualifier in 2012 and you'll know exactly what I mean.

A couple of times during filming he became impatient and took his microphone off. Stewart and I had a signal to carry on filming anyway. So much of the footage that was taken when he didn't think he was being filmed was better than when he was 'acting', so to speak, but the bleep machine was working overtime. We knew he hated flying, so we smuggled the camera on as hand luggage so we could witness him at take-off. His suffering and anxiety made great TV!

It was obvious he was loved in Malta; everyone we met on the streets of Valetta hugged him. I'm not saying he's a national hero like an Edward de Bono or composer Charles Camilleri, but people do respect what he has done and achieved and how he has promoted his country.

The reunion with his mother was especially emotional; she raised him almost single-handedly and dotes on him to this day. When Tony states that if you say 'bad' about his mother you are a dead man, there is not one hint of sarcasm in his voice. I knew if I kept asking the right questions about her he would eventually get emotional.

I think the documentary was quite cathartic for him. By speaking in depth for the first time about his childhood, he really opened up. I also think it made him sad that a career of 25 years as one of Malta's top sportsmen had still left him needing to earn money to find each month's rent.

Tony has never been married, and to my knowledge never had a long-term girlfriend: his two loves are his mother and food. Looking at early pictures of Tony, he was as thin as a rake; loneliness in those early years in the UK was comforted with over-eating.

He was good company and we got great footage. I also interviewed Jimmy White and pool player Raj Hundal for the programme. We finished the filming at the 2014 Legends Cup and shortly after that it was released on our app.

The response was good; we were only charging 99p for it. Then it got picked up by TVM1 in Malta, the equivalent of the BBC over here. We made a few quid, Tony made a few quid; happy days. I've made it free now, partly because making money from it was never the main reason, but also because I think it's a good thing to have out there on my CV. It cost literally nothing to make but I think it stands up alongside plenty of sporting documentaries I have watched.

I tried to help Tony, a bit in the same way I tried to help Alex. Now, I am not comparing their characters, but they are similar in the way that if you can get to the real Tony you see a guy who means well but has lost his way a bit.

In some ways the documentary needs a new ending; we need to go back and speak with Tony three years on from where we left off. He's back in Valetta now, no longer a professional snooker player, unemployed and living back in his bedroom. We've got him a bit involved in the World Seniors Tour; he is talented enough to win it, for sure.

The most extreme tornadoes can attain wind speeds of more than 300 miles per hour; they are unpredictable. Who's to say tornado Tony won't touch down again one day and remind us just how destructive he can be at the table? Fun and torture at the same time is guaranteed, plus, I expect, a little bit of bad language.

CHAPTER 29

2014 SEASON, ALL CHANGE

When the ratings came through from Eurosport we'd achieved viewing figures of 12.3 million, which was staggering. Of course you have to put it in context, but when you consider that more people watched the Legends Cup across Europe than watched an episode of *The X-Factor* in the UK, I was pretty chuffed.

Our ratings were better than those reported for most PTCs. I couldn't help thinking this was the start of an extended run of TV broadcasts where I would actually get paid for the product I had created. Sadly I was wrong.

On two separate occasions I got a letter of intent from Eurosport regarding a new broadcast. I even sat with the big bosses in Paris to discuss resurrecting and producing the World Trick Shot Championship for them. It always came down to money. They were getting offered sport for free: figure skating was one example that was always used against me: 'Why should we pay for snooker when we get figure skating for free?'

I didn't understand the comparison then and I don't now, save for a joke about a few players skating on thin ice.

One person who did like what we did was JK, chairman at the ROK Group, and in the words of Victor Kiam from the old Remington adverts, 'liked it so much I bought the company!'

Within a month or so of the Legends Cup I accepted an offer to sell half of the Snooker Legends brand to 'Events that ROK' and took up the CEO's position with a stakeholding in that company. It was a massive move for me but one that I felt would finally give me the resources to expand and try out new ideas. JK invests in people. He loved the idea of having someone like me on board to develop both our ideas.

Within a few weeks I had Ronnie, Jimmy, Michaela and a film crew in a barn just outside Telford trying out my first idea: 6 Red Pool.

I'd been aware of feedback from America that a frame of snooker took just too long to make an impact on the audiences there. They loved the skill of snooker but not the time it took – hence why you'll never see cricket played much over the pond.

Basically, 6 Red Pool was snooker with six reds played on an American 9 ball table with 9-ball-sized balls. It was quick but also had skill. The maximum break was 75 and the idea was to play matches over longer formats, for example first to 20 racks.

Jimmy liked it, or he certainly liked the idea of the extra work it could bring in. Ronnie wasn't so sure. JK at ROK loved the idea and the format was put forward for consideration for a TV show in America called *Billion Dollar Brand*. Basically this was a version of the UK's *Dragons' Den* but hosted by a billionaire called John Paul DeJoria – who just happened to be a shareholder in ROK Stars. John Paul had already created two billion-dollar brands – Paul Mitchell Haircare and Patrón Tequila – and the programme was about his search for a third.

We did the promotional video, Michaela helped write the

rules, and I tried out the game at my local club. It was quick, neat, and kids liked it.

I was due to go to America in December 2013 to film for *Billion Dollar Brand*. However, it never happened – I kept being told it was just delayed. I felt a bit of blagging was going on.

6 Red Pool sits protected, ready for the day when we may get the backing to try it out. Will it ever happen? I'd like to think so, but I don't know. It was frustrating to say the least.

Two things that were going ahead were the Drago documentary and the creation of the Snooker Legends App.

ROK had the skilled personnel and track record of building apps for mobile devices. The idea was that if we couldn't broadcast our events we would stream them via pay-per-view into our own app.

I already had a lot of content, hours of previous Legends shows. We could launch the app with a free download; we could then earn revenues from selling 'in app' purchases and our pay-per-view events. I also had hundreds of event photos. It was a project that wasn't going to take much of my time, and any money it brought in was a bonus.

Show-wise we had another great night in Belfast. Ronnie was on the bill, and they signed autographs for nearly two hours. We also welcomed 1986 World Champion Joe Johnson to the team in Plymouth, and made him bring the pink shoes he was famous for wearing the year he won. We also returned to Liverpool for a show, and ITV came along and filmed part of their *Sports Life Stories* programme on Jimmy at the event.

Ronnie played in Southend, another sell-out, but his Legends appearances were now being restricted by his new manager, a bloke put in place by Ronnie's dad, despite having no previous experience.

When this guy first started with Ronnie he badgered me constantly for information and contacts. Daily phone calls asking how to do this, how is this done, do you know this person? I obliged because I thought I was helping Ronnie, then suddenly when it came to booking Ronnie for shows this guy increased Ronnie's appearance fees by 300 per cent. Thanks very much: when will I ever learn?

It meant that for much of this time I concentrated on shows with my staple four: Jimmy, Hendry, Davis and Taylor – a proven quartet who always delivered entertainment and were no trouble.

For our annual visit to the Crucible in April in 2014 I was restricted to only using non-contracted players, so once again I couldn't book Jimmy or Steve. I had Stephen of course, and used JP again, his first visit since 2011. I also took Tony Knowles and Joe Johnson back there. The show sold OK but it wasn't sold out; there is no doubt the line-up was missing a Jimmy, Davis or Ronnie.

However, for this showcase event I'd introduced a 'VVIP', which was one step up from the VIP we did! In truth I made it up. The players laughed at my guile but this package included a backstage tour of the Crucible with a legend and a chance to play on the table with Stephen. They also got their photo taken with the World Trophy. Add in the overnight hotel and I sold the 20 slots easily. Stephen was wondering what I would come up with next!

My mate Andy came up to the Crucible and won the raffle to play that night – people said it was fixed, but I had nothing to do with it. I actually own a snooker club in Newbury with Andy and a guy named Lyndon, called…The Crucible Sports and Social Club.

I'd tried plenty of different merchandise lines; again, some of the random items I used to sell had the legends shaking their heads in disbelief, or was it admiration? Cuff links, mouse mats, coasters and my particular favourites… fridge magnets! We also did iPhone covers: we sold them, but I quickly realised that Apple changed their phone designs too often to make it viable.

I decided to stream the Crucible event live into the app. We did it for free to try it out and as I had no contracted players; World Snooker couldn't stop me doing it. This was more about testing the technology ready for the streaming of our Legends Cup, which was taking place a month later.

Another guest, and a way of selling more tickets, was a seven-year-old lad I'd seen at an exhibition with Jimmy. Young Westley Cooper from Leicester wasn't tall enough to reach the table, so he stood on a box that he trailed behind him. I say it was a box, but it was actually a bread tray. It was hilarious, but this kid was talented and I reckoned in about another ten years I'd be selling that footage to the BBC when he plays in the main championships. It started out as a one-frame challenge match against Stephen, then Stephen potted a ball and got booed; he said it felt like he was back playing Jimmy again!

Snooker Legends had given one young boy the chance to play in the Crucible. That could never have happened before our shows and it's moments like that, and taking the former players back there, that make it all worthwhile.

Another ace up my sleeve was that for the 2014 World Championship Ronnie went out wearing my logo, the Snooker Legends App. We got 30,000 downloads – it was perfect advertising. Just as the Eurosport broadcast was a big moment, so was this. The defending World Snooker champion, and world's most popular player, was going out live on the BBC wearing my brand.

We almost had the fairy-tale ending as well, and I truly believe one black ball off the spot at 10-6 up cost Ronnie the title. But fair play to Mark Selby: never has the World Championship been won by someone who battled for it, or indeed wanted it, more.

For the 2014 Legends Cup I decided to announce new captains and it was Dennis and Cliff who had to make way. Jimmy would captain England and his nemesis Stephen the Rest of the World.

Steve Davis and Ronnie were givens for Jimmy's team but I

took a punt and booked the ladies' World Snooker Champion, Reanne Evans. I knew she could play, and commercially I thought it was a good move. I was also frustrated that she was largely unrecognised in the game and I think had got lost with a previous management team who had 20-plus players to look after, most of whom were delivering more commission than Reanne was.

For Stephen's team I booked Drago – his MVP performance a year earlier made that an easy one, and it was a good chance to get footage for the documentary – then I went for Mark Williams from Wales and a controversial selection, Dechawat Poomjaeng, from Thailand. 'The Poom', as he was known, was a madcap player who had made a real name for himself at the previous World Championship with his antics.

People loved him but I got criticised on social media. 'He's not a legend,' they said. I had to remind them that he was, in fact, a former World Amateur Champion and a superstar in Thailand. We were streaming worldwide, so I thought I could capitalise on that.

I got my World Snooker sanction; again, as I met all the criteria, they couldn't really turn me down. We were charging £2.99 for the whole two days' stream booked upfront, or £4.99 if you booked on the day.

I also left Bedworth behind and went to a new venue, The Hexagon Theatre in Reading. It was one I had used before, and it has a history of staging tournaments. We'd done well before with shows there and I'd been working with the venue since 1997, but once again sales were slow, despite me having eight players with 30 world titles between them.

Then to top it off there was a military coup in Thailand which prevented 'The Poom' getting his visa to come to the UK. Not for the first time, I had player problems just 24 hours before the event. I got on the phone to Ken Doherty; he got on a plane at short notice and answered the call for the Rest of the World.

Looking at the teams, I once again found it difficult to decide who I thought would win. Sure, England had the world champion in Ronnie, but analysing the other three, Steve had fallen off-tour, Jimmy had just clung on to his tour place, and Reanne had never beaten a top pro in a ranking tournament.

For the Rest of the World you could argue Stephen would be rusty, but in Mark and Ken you still had two top performers, and with the way Drago approached these tournaments, I made them favourites.

How wrong I was. Jimmy's team dished out the biggest hiding I have ever seen. In the first match both Jimmy and Reanne had century breaks, Reanne's a beautiful 117 clearance where she took the final blue left-handed, the pink right-handed and the black one-handed. She made an immediate impression, and playing in front of a big crowd seemed to inspire her. The only player to show any fight for Stephen's team was Mark Williams, who weighed in with two centuries himself.

The match was over by the start of the fourth session: England had won 18-3. We played out the matches as a courtesy to the fans that were there but we never got any black-ball finishes. Reanne won the MVP award; as well as her centuries, she was undefeated in the doubles, and had also beaten Drago and Ken in singles matches. Ronnie didn't drop a frame all tournament and made the tournament high break, a 133.

We did have Eurosport with us, but only to film an episode of *The Ronnie O'Sullivan Show*. I gave them full access to everything in return for a pledge that Ronnie would interview Reanne. By now I'd reached a deal with her to take over her management and my search for tour sponsorship for her had begun. It also sowed the seed I'd use to get her her first stint as a pundit with Eurosport during the 2017 UK Champs.

That summer we took the show to the Isle of Man and also Inverness in Scotland. I could sense it was becoming harder to sell tickets. In some ways my reliance on Ronnie for full houses was becoming greater than ever.

In September Ronnie asked me to find him a proper management to start developing his global profile and prepare for a career when he no longer played tournament snooker. It seems he had finally seen what most of us had realised months earlier – namely that the choice he had made with his current manager was a huge mistake.

After one show, he came up to me to congratulate me on the tickets sold, but then informed me that I had to change the cloth, since in his opinion it just wasn't right for Ronnie to play on the one we were using. I said I would give him three guesses to tell me what cloth we were actually using that night, and if he got it right I'd change it. He soon shut up.

He also asked me to approach Ronnie's former manager, Django, to see if he wanted to sell his Academy where Ronnie still practised. Looking back, I can't believe I did it, but he told me Ronnie was aware of the idea and it didn't make sense for Ronnie to be practising in a venue owned by his former manager. The truth was he was jealous and insecure that Ronnie would go back to Django. A few months later I had to smooth it over with Django. He must have thought I was a right idiot for trying to buy his Academy when I now lived over a hundred miles from it. Ronnie had no idea.

Another crazy idea this manager had was to create a new official website and then charge fans to join it. It was complete madness. By offering them a signed photo and exclusive access to blogs and online chats, something Ronnie was never going to do, he felt he could charge people £19.99. Some people did sign up and two years later I was tasked with having to try to refund people and manage the negative feedback from those fans who'd handed over money.

Back in 2005 I wrote the stage show for a children's TV programme called *Engie Benjy*. The two main characters were voiced by Ant and Dec and they agreed to record the stage show for me. This brought me into contact with their managers, who were called James Grant. Now James Grant isn't a person but the middle names of the agency's founders, Russ Lindsay and Peter Powell – yes, he of Radio 1 DJ fame.

At this time they were a fairly small agency; now they are London's largest and still look after Ant and Dec, as well as stars like Keith Lemon, Phillip Schofield, Davina McCall and people from sport like Neil Warnock, Clint Dempsey and England cricketer Jonny Bairstow. I thought they would be perfect for Ronnie and so called up my contact from that time, a lady called Ali Astall, who became Dec's wife in 2016.

I took Ronnie in for two meetings with James Grant; they weren't desperate to grab him and that was actually a good thing for him. They only wanted to work with him if they felt they could make a difference, and they were aware of a reputation Ronnie had for not turning up to tournaments.

I did a lot of work behind the scenes with them and met them on more than one occasion on my own. I was convinced they were right for him, plus of course it meant he would get rid of the previous manager. Ronnie signed and I became, for the short term, the 'snooker advisor' to James Grant. I was back travelling with Ronnie to tournaments and at the first one I returned for, the Champion of Champions in Coventry, Ronnie won and walked away with a cheque for £100,000.

I was quickly able to book new shows with Ronnie and start concentrating on my next big project, the Irish Legends Cup. A tournament that would pitch Ireland v England, in Dublin. Fair to say, that would get the juices flowing.

During this season it was decided that World Snooker would no longer run any Player Tour Championship events in the UK. These events were now regarded as more of a second tier but they did attract a lot of the top amateurs. I decided to create my own style of PTC, and so the Snooker Legends Pro-Am series was born.

One benefit of this was I could stage it at my own club. The idea was to get 64 amateurs to play on the Saturday down to 16 qualifiers and then invite 16 pros to join them on the Sunday. It meant that club amateurs could win two matches and get a dream tie against a pro, with 21 points a frame start.

I lined up my 16 pros. I was able to get Jimmy, Stuart Bingham and Tony Drago easily, and then of course could add in Reanne and a few other pros I had met at that time, such as Michael Wasley and Barry Pinches. I was delighted when fellow pros Mark Davis, Rob Milkins, Ben Woollaston and Jimmy Robertson contacted me. The event was a great success, and from a networking point of view I got to meet many of the top amateurs too.

It was won by then amateur, now professional, Daniel Wells, who carried off £1,200. We had ten centuries in the weekend. Amateurs really enjoyed getting to hang out with the professionals and we did a few Crucible Burgers that day too! A few local amateurs took a pro scalp as well: those club tables are certainly a leveller.

The Pro-Am series is something else that I thought I would develop further. I staged two more of them, won by Mark King and Zak Surety. The problem then was that I simply became too busy to do more.

I've never been more involved in snooker and yet I've never actually played less than I do now. I'd love to be able to play in one of my events; one day, with an independent tournament director, maybe I will. The middle of the white can't be too hard to find again after all this time... can it?

CHAPTER 30

THE IRISH LEGENDS CUP

After three years of keeping the Legends Cup the same, and, if I'm going to be honest, prompted by low ticket sales in Reading, I decided to rework the event and stage the 2015 one in Ireland.

The venue was easy: the horse-sales' ring in County Kildare, known as Goffs. Back in the 1980s and 1990s Goffs was the home for the Benson & Hedges Irish Masters, and it is a venue quite like no other, with the table sitting in a tight circular area with the crowd in close all the way round. With steep seating the atmosphere was electric there, as was the legendary hospitality. Benson & Hedges piled lots of money into the event. It was hard for a member of the general public to get seats as they were mostly gifted to the corporate partners of Phillip Morris, the brand owners.

For Bensons the snooker was really a sideshow; the hospitality enjoyed by the chairman of somewhere like Tesco ensured that orders were placed for millions of cigarettes over that week for the following year. I'm not sure you'd get away with it nowadays, but getting your quota of product into these outlets was big business and well worth the cost of staging the tournament. Also, of course, any player who played in the tournament left there with a lorry load of fags, a gift from the sponsor. Players were encouraged to smoke; if you could associate your brand with someone like Jimmy White or Alex Higgins then that had a real value... until of course the next tournament, when a new sponsor like Rothmans or Embassy was handing out the cigs! In the 1980s plenty of top-16 players always had some cheap smokes for sale if you had the reddies to hand.

Nowadays, once a player loses, he is in his car and down the motorway as quickly as he can; for the Irish Masters tournament you had to stay till the end, irrespective of when you got beaten. Finals were staged with many of the other top players in their evening suits sitting in the front row for the cameras, there as a guest of Mr Asda or Mr Morrison. It was all about the image.

I first took snooker back to Goffs in 2011. I'm still the only promoter using it to this day. When it's full of snooker fans it truly is a remarkable place to be. If I needed to stoke up the atmosphere any more then why not pitch Ireland against England? It had only been 900 years since the Norman Invasion and let's not forget the involvement of the Earl of Kildare, titled after the county in which we were staging the match. He was well versed for putting down the English rebellion in his time!

After he demolished Stephen's team in Reading, Jimmy wanted to captain England again and take the same team to Ireland. Steve Davis and Reanne committed immediately, but Ronnie wanted to see what access he was getting to his kids over Christmas. That was understandable as the event fell between Christmas and New Year; I was sympathetic to his priorities but still disappointed.

I turned to Ali Carter. If ever there was an inspirational English snooker player to replace the Rocket, it was going to be him. First he had coped with Crohn's disease, then he had testicular cancer, the same as Jimmy, and he'd only just recovered from a form of lung cancer to play again. I knew that the Irish fans would welcome him with open arms, even though he was on the opposing team: they love and admire a true battler.

For Ireland I decided to go the way of the old Nations Cup and pull from both Northern Ireland and Eire. So in reality it was All Ireland.

Ken Doherty was captain, a former world champion, and with the nickname the 'Darlin' of Dublin' it was an obvious choice. Ken also has other nicknames, 'Crafty Ken' is one and 'Careful Ken' is another. I'm not sure if the 'Careful' is in any way related to the story where shortly after his 1997 World Championship Victory, where he pocketed a cool £210,000, he rewarded his car with a new set of remoulded tyres!

I brought back Dennis Taylor – after Alex Higgins, he is Northern Ireland's most decorated player – and then I was stuck with choosing from a possible three other candidates for the two remaining berths.

Fergal O'Brien is the only player who has ever phoned me and almost begged to be included. In fact, I probably could have got him to play for nothing! Being a local lad, within a stone's throw of Goffs, he was desperate to represent his country; he also pledged to work hard to sell tickets for me. Fergal was in, and with hindsight never had I made a better decision.

So it came down to a choice between Mark Allen and Joe Swail. Rankings-wise it was a no-brainer; Mark is regarded as one of the top ten players in the world and a multiple event winner. Joe has been around for a while, so certainly qualifies for Legends status, and people forget he has made two semi-finals at the Crucible.

The fly in the ointment, and one that clouded my judgement, was a little girl called Lauren. Lauren is the daughter of Reanne Evans and Mark Allen, and it's a broken relationship. They barely speak. Since I had become Reanne's manager it now meant there was an emotional involvement. However, the devil in me, the event-maker, thought that having Mark on the Ireland team and Reanne on the England team would be electric. Nothing sells better than controversy.

I spoke to Reanne and told her that commercially I should be booking Mark and that we'd exchanged messages on Twitter, and he was up for playing. Michaela also said that he was excellent with people in exhibitions, another quality we look for on these shows.

Reanne said she wouldn't feel comfortable with him being there, so I stayed loyal to her and did a deal with Joe. It was the right decision to make as the manager of Reanne; it was probably the wrong decision to make commercially for Snooker Legends and the event.

The launch dinner was being taken out of my hands. I'd sold it to a colleague of Ken's who had booked the Mansion House in Dublin and was going to stage a charity event. I knew the amount I usually made for the dinner, which was money that went towards the prize money and hotel costs at the event. Of course I could never guarantee I would make money, so selling the event was an easy decision.

I started getting nervous about the event in October when the guy wasn't coming back to me with final details. Also, I was offering to help him sell tickets so found it strange he wasn't engaging. All the players' flights and hotels had been booked around arriving on Sunday 28th and attending the event that night.

When he finally did get in touch he admitted he'd paid a 5K deposit for the Mansion House on the Saturday, not the Sunday. He'd messed up the dates and was struggling to sell tables. He blamed Ken for saying the Saturday.

I always incentivise all the guys to earn if they bring sponsors to the table, so Ken was on a commission for delivering this. I'm not sure if he was earning a bit the other end as well. Either way it was a mess and the guy had to cancel the dinner. It seemed as though problems with the Legends Cup just seemed to crop up wherever I played it.

Staging a three-day event is a major operation; staging it in another country makes it costly and logistically tricky. I was nervous that without Ronnie the event could struggle to sell enough tickets to cover costs. I thought having it so close after Christmas would mean we'd sell lots of tickets as presents. In the lead-up to the event I almost dreaded getting the reports from Ticketmaster – with a month to go the sales were woefully short of my break-even point.

I'm old and ugly enough to know that putting on any event is a risk. I'd been badly burnt in Reading in the May, but I'd like to think not one player ever knew exactly the trouble I got into – £50,000 worth of trouble. Selling the tickets and promoting the event is my job. I don't treat the event or players any differently if I am making or losing money. You will never hear me go to a player after an event and ask him to take a smaller fee because I have lost money; that's not my style. Then again, I don't go opening the chequebook to offer them extra when I've made it either, so it works both ways.

As I said earlier, the thing I admire about Barry Hearn, and something he tells me is mutual, is that he's put his hands in his pockets and risked personal money. It takes balls to do that. As my good friend Neil tells me, 'Sometimes it works and sometimes it doesn't. The key is not to feel either way about it.'

By the first week of December, tickets started to pick up: I was selling 20 to 30 a day. Fergal O'Brien must have sold me near on 100 tickets easy; he worked so hard to promote the event. In some ways if all the other guys showed the same commitment to making the event a success as he did then, I could sit back stress-free. Fergal, you'll do for me on any future event like this in Ireland.

The launch of Jimmy's second autobiography meant he had a promotional trip to Dublin two weeks before our show; it was a perfect chance to join him and turn it into a PR event for the Legends Cup as well. We caught the red-eye flight out of Heathrow and by 8am we were sat having breakfast in Bewleys

Hotel in Dublin doing his first interview. We probably did 10–12 interviews that day, plus a book signing in Eason's.

Jimmy was superb. We laughed at how 20 years before he'd have never made that flight or had the patience to sit answering the same questions over and over again. At every interview he would plug the Legends; we also met up with Ken and did a great interview for his radio station that had come on board as a partner. We went to RTE and bumped into Nicky Byrne from Westlife. Everyone loved Jimmy; truthfully, I'm not even sure he understands why.

As is customary with every Legends Cup we've done, there was a last-minute player drama. At the first Legends Cup Ronnie was over the limit, at the second Neil missed the dinner, and at the third 'The Poom', Dechawat Poomjaeng, was stuck in Thailand while a military coup went on... This time my mate Michaela was ill.

I was getting nervous leading up to Goffs because she was still off sick with World Snooker. On the 9th December I had no choice but to send her the following email:

Hi Michaela,
I hope you are well. I've put off sending this email,
because as you know I think the world of you but I need
to ask if you think you are going to be well enough to
referee at Legends Cup in Goffs in a few weeks. I notice
I haven't had your contract back, in truth I'd missed
checking for it as we've worked together for so long. I'm
aware you haven't been at World Snooker events and the
reason is none of my business, but I hope you understand I
need to make sure I don't get left with only Trish.

If you feel you can't attend, for whatever reason, can
you let me know so I can approach Jan. I'm sorry to have
to send this email but I hope you understand why.
Jason x

I felt bad about sending the email but I knew she would understand. After me she cares more about the Snooker Legends brand than anyone else. She did eventually phone to tell me she wasn't well enough to come; I was gutted that she wouldn't be with us in Ireland.

Once I knew, we turned to Jan Verhaas, who had worked at the previous few Legends Cups and was one of the team. He'd fit in perfectly. Jan was the referee for Ronnie's record tenth maximum break in 2010 at the World Open. After finding out that there was no special prize for completing a 147, Ron shook hands with opponent Mark King after potting the last pink. Jan, however, persuaded the Rocket to pot the last black and finish his break.

Jan had recently married a lady from Belarus called Lena. Jan would have loved to do the Cup, but Lena's passport meant she couldn't travel into Ireland. It was their first married Christmas together; I couldn't expect him to leave her. We did get her to Dublin in 2018 but didn't see much of her as she got a bug that decimated the whole group.

I talked to Michaela about who we could use instead. Patricia Murphy was already there, and had experience of Legends, but she hadn't officiated at the top level for years because she'd almost retired to bring up her young family. Michaela was adamant I needed an A-band referee; her choice was Belgian Olivier Marteel, a top-class referee who took charge of the PTC finals but hadn't yet got a major final. Within the space of a couple of emails the deal was done and we had booked Olivier.

It was a great choice. Olivier added calm when the crowd got going, and trust me, as you will read later, they certainly got going! He was a joy to work with; nothing was too much trouble and I think he had a great time. I'm now blessed with lots of great referees on my team. Olivier has taken charge of the Worlds and Masters since Goffs.

We all arrived in Dublin on 27th December, via one of the

worst ferry crossings you can imagine! We had a long set-up day at the venue whilst the players descended on the town of Naas in County Kildare from all over Europe. Instead of the launch dinner we did our own dinner where the wine flowed, everyone relaxed, and the captains announced their line-ups for the first day.

Jimmy put himself and Steve out first and they got paired against Ken and Fergal. That meant Reanne and Ali played Joe and Dennis. In the singles Ali was to play Ken, Jimmy was against Fergal, Reanne v Dennis, and Steve battling Joe.

The English boys got straight into Dennis: 'No one wants to lose to a girl!' they jibed. Reanne wasn't bothered; after all, she was the one saying it to him! The banter and wind-ups had well and truly begun. It was game on!

CHAPTER 31

THE BATTLE OF KILDARE

Over the breakfast table on Day 1 the talk was all about which team would win. On paper Ireland had three players ranked in the top 64 – England only had two – plus, of course, they were playing at home. Ken had described the Goffs crowd as his Fifth Man, but the reality is, Jimmy is loved as much in Ireland as any of the lads who'd be going out in the green shirts. It was a close call, for sure.

Jimmy said the key would be how his team performed in the singles matches. Doubles are always a lottery, and quite often the strongest player on paper can easily be shut out. Then of course the format I'd created meant that if a doubles match went one-frame-all then it was settled with a black ball re-spot, which is a complete lottery.

We had a good crowd in – not spectacular, but it was Monday afternoon and quite a few people had already started back at work. I could sense the new players didn't really know what to expect: was this an exhibition or was it serious? My only advice was it needed to be entertaining – that was the thing that had set us apart from anyone else, and every player needed to buy into it and play their part.

There were six points on offer in the first session. Jimmy wanted three, convinced that Ireland would come out strong.

The Whirlwind had purposely put himself in the first match. He got a huge reception and led by example, slamming in a quick-fire 63 break to take the first frame. Fergal responded in frame two with 65. We were already into our first black-ball shoot-out of the competition and it was only two o'clock!

Before the match Team Ireland had been at the table working out how to play the re-spots. It was their opinion that the top cushion would 'square up', so attempting a long treble was preferable to a double.

As so often in his career, Jimmy ripped up the rule book and promptly doubled the black in. First blood to England. If the new lads didn't know what the Legends Cup was all about before, they certainly did now.

Ali Carter got a great reception when he came down for match two and responded with a 73, three frames and three single-visit breaks – the standard was high. The second frame was scrappy, but Reanne made some important balls and it was a simple victory for them: 2-0.

It was clear that Joe and Dennis hadn't yet got their arms going, but Ken reassured them that it was going to be a long two days and everyone would play their part.

Into the singles: Ken was playing England's top ranked player, Ali Carter, and you had to favour the man from Essex. Captain Ken fired in a fantastic 107. It would end up being the highest break of the tournament, but more importantly it was 2-1. Ireland was on the board. Then Jimmy got himself 34 up with one red left on the table, but Fergal cleared with 35 and celebrated like he'd already won the Cup. The crowd loved it, Fergal was pumped and Ireland were back level.

Dennis did get beaten by 'the girl' in the next match but he wasn't guilty of playing badly. The truth is Reanne was just too good. Jimmy had his three points; anything from the last match from the Nugget was going to be a bonus.

Despite being ranked so much lower than Joe, Steve was much more used to playing in front of a big crowd. He won and Jimmy's England had a 4-2 lead. Reanne and Steve were undefeated.

During the break Dennis and Joe were out at the practice table. Joe confided he was nervous, explaining he hadn't played in front of such a big crowd for quite some time. It was something I hadn't really considered but so much snooker is played nowadays in front of one man and his dog. Then again, Joe had played in two Crucible semi-finals; it's amazing how they can quickly forget how to perform under pressure.

Between sessions we all dined on roast beef and chicken, and I'm pretty sure it tasted better if you were wearing the blue shirt of England.

DAY 1, SESSION 2
England: 4; All Ireland: 2

The evening's doubles started with Fergal and Joe taking on Jimmy and Ali. Once again this was a key match for Ireland, and they didn't want to drop three points behind in this race to 18.

Ali Carter made 50 in the first frame, and an Irish victory looked unlikely. Suddenly 'The Outlaw' Joe Swail got in the balls and ran a beautiful 82 break; it was just what he needed to settle him down. Once again we had a re-spotted black, with Ken watching from the balcony urging the boys on.

After about three attempts Joe was left with a long black and Olivier called for hush. Joe seemed to cue up for ages, but his technique held strong and he made the ball. The crowd cheered, but more importantly the score was back to 3-2 and Joe Swail could relax. He'd made his first significant contribution to the team.

The next doubles match with Steve, Reanne, Ken and Dennis had just the 18 world titles on show; it was the 1997 Darlin' of Dublin who took the frame with an 88 break.

Steve Davis responded and cleared the colours to make it 1-1 and the old black ball was put up again. This time it was Ken who doubled it. He celebrated by calling for more noise from the crowd. He wasn't disappointed: 4-4.

When we started the singles, Fergal beat Jimmy, then Ali beat Joe. The match between Reanne and Ken looked on paper as though it should go Ken's way, but it was the Ladies world champion who won it. Jimmy was thrilled: she had won her second singles match of the day.

Ali was looking tired and asked to go back to the hotel. I always knew two long days were going to be tough for him. Sure, he was elated at being given the all-clear only a week before Christmas, but the effects of months of chemotherapy meant he was far from fighting fit. Jimmy jumped in the taxi, too; I think he was more hanging from the night before than actually tired!

The final match of Day 1 was a repeat of the 1985 final. We hadn't rigged the draw in any way but it was a great match-up. Steve and Dennis have replayed that frame so many times in exhibitions, they have a script that works and is very funny. That night, all the gags were forgotten. This was probably the most serious frame they had played against each other since that night in Sheffield 30 years ago. I thought this could be their last match-up together, until of course Steve replaced Hendry at the Irish Masters in 2018 and drew... Dennis.

It was a pretty turgid frame until Steve got in and cleared with a very impressive 57. England led overnight. When I got back to the bar almost all the players were in bed, even though they weren't playing until 1pm the next day. They had seen enough to know they didn't want to be the person who let their team down.

Dennis was pretty down: he hadn't played well that day and

his pride in performance was refreshing for me. Here was a guy with nothing to prove to anyone, yet it still mattered. I loved that.

The overnight frost made it a very fresh morning in Naas. I knew we had a long day ahead and I thought this one could go right to the wire. When the young table-fitter Kieran asked me if we rigged the score to keep it close, you can imagine how that went down with Jimmy. In Thorburn's words, shots were being played like they were for pints of blood. This was more important than money.

DAY 2, SESSION 3
England: 7; All Ireland 5

Ali and Steve took the first frame of the session and 8-5 looked likely, but once again Ireland refused to lie down and Ken and Joe pinched the next frame. Then Joe nailed another re-spot and Ireland were back to 7-6.

Reanne was impressive in the next match, clearing with 54, the last black her trademark one-handed. I think it riled Fergal a bit: was she showboating? Maybe it was his way of motivating himself; it certainly worked, as his clearance in the next frame forced another black-ball decider. Fergal stayed in the zone and duly potted the black again to get it back to 7-7. From now on it was going to be singles.

In the interval Ken had to list his playing order for the final session. All of Team Ireland were locked away for a full ten minutes trying to guess which way Jimmy would go. By this time Stephen Hendry had arrived to see his girlfriend Lauren who works on our shows, and he couldn't believe how seriously they were all taking it.

First up was Ali against Dennis. It was closer than perhaps it should have been as Dennis came to the table 65 behind and made five reds and five blacks. Down to the yellow and Ali fluked it. JV said to the crowd, 'Ali has had a bit of luck there.' Ali quipped back, 'I think I'm due a bit, don't you?' The crowd all applauded. Hard to argue with that one.

It was 8-7 but many expected Fergal to beat Steve to make it 8-8, especially when the Irishman had a 30-point lead with just the colours left. Steve laid a great snooker, got the four-point foul and promptly cleared up. A critical frame pinched and it was 9-7. Fergal looked stern.

Captain Ken won the next match, defeating Jimmy, then Joe beat Reanne – her first singles defeat. Amazingly it was 9-9!

The session was overrunning, so we had to delay the start time for the final matches by 30 minutes; good job as the place was heaving and we only had standing room in Goffs. Eight singles and eight points were on offer but we knew we'd be going to final black balls as neither team could get to the winning post of 18.

DAY 2, FINAL SESSION

England: 9; All Ireland: 9

The reception the players received for the final session gave everyone goosebumps. Quite a few players said they had never heard anything like it. Just before Ken was called on I slipped him the Irish tricolour. He draped it around his shoulders and the crowd took the roof off. I'd chosen 'The Irish Rover' by the Pogues to bring on the Irish team and it worked perfectly.

It was like a pressure cooker in there. Almost every player not playing was either on the balcony or out in the crowd, save Steve Davis who watched from the players' room, glued to his iPad, probably playing chess or listening to techno.

Jimmy played perhaps his best frame of the event to beat Ken, which put extra pressure on Fergal, as it was his turn to play Reanne.

During the break in play he asked me if he had to kiss Reanne before the match started. I must have looked quizzically at him, but he explained that he was there to beat her not kiss her and be all friendly. That would be for afterwards. He was so in the zone the last thing he wanted was to have any friendly feelings for his opponent. It wasn't disrespectful in any way; it was just a statement of how much he wanted to win.

That focus got him 60 ahead, but then he let Reanne in and she took all the balls to the brown, leaving her 21 behind with 22 on. She rattled the brown; it was sitting over the hole, but in this atmosphere nothing was easy. I was really proud how our referees allowed the crowd to be supportive and loud but kept them quiet on the key shots. Fergal overcut the brown. He will claim it drifted, but either way Reanne pounced to clear up.

Everyone was stunned. England once more had a two-point lead!

There were only about 20 steps out of the arena back to the players' lounge but the way the players climbed those steps was fascinating. Those who had won were giving the high fives all the way, savouring every moment of victory with the crowd. If you lost you were scuttling up the stairs, shoulders hunched and head down, save Steve Davis of course… I never had any idea whether he'd won or lost a frame – the Nugget, eh?

Being two points behind, Joe had a crucial match-up with Ali. Again in a normal ranker you would make Joe only a 5/6-1 shot. But once again the Outlaw dug deep for his country and drew them back to 11-10. Steve Davis won the last of the session, again beating Dennis, so going into the final session it was 12-10 to England. With just four singles to play, Ireland badly needed three of them.

Social media was buzzing. Ali tweeted: 'Final Session tonight in the snooker legends in front of a packed house! So happy to be here with my health intact, love you all xxx'

Even then I had a funny feeling Ali would have a pivotal role in the outcome of this tournament.

On Twitter Mark Williams was demanding he captain a Welsh team to challenge. The world of snooker was getting involved in the event at Goffs, and more importantly for me, they were getting involved in a Snooker Legends event.

Ken beat Davis. 12-11 now, the fight-back was on… However, it was to be the last singles frame England would win, with Reanne defeating Joe, Jimmy beating Dennis, and Ali clearing to win a tight one with Fergal.

Everyone took a breath. The climax I always plan for was about to happen. All eight players entered the arena. England needed to win three re-spots, Ireland needed seven, which was a big ask.

England took the first two black balls. Surely it was all over?

Then Ireland turned to the black-ball specialist Dennis Taylor, and he duly delivered a cross double to keep Emerald Isle dreams alive. The noise inside Goffs was deafening; sure it was mostly Irish support, but it was impossible not to get caught up in it.

I stood alone behind the play. A smile broke out on my face: it was for moments like this that I had put in months and months of work.

Ken potted an almost impossible thin black to give Ireland one more point.

At 17-14 Jimmy turned to Ali. He knew just one pot would win the Cup – and how fitting would it be for the man who had battled lung cancer earlier this year, and won the biggest battle of all, to enjoy a moment of triumph on the table.

Fergal won the toss and put Ali in. The crowd went quiet… He attempted a full-length double into the yellow pocket. By the time the black hit the top cushion all of the England team had run across to judge the path of the black… and they began celebrating while it was more than three feet out.

Cancer survivor Ali Carter had potted the ball that saw England retain the Legends Cup. The final score: 18-14.

The champagne corks popped too early, much to the relief

of the table fitters who didn't want it all over the cloth, but no one minded.

I thanked a few people, especially JV, and pledged to return to Goffs again. This tussle deserved a rematch. Did I decide that on the spur of the moment in the emotion of it all? Of course not: I'd decided it when I saw the full house a few hours earlier. There is definitely money to be made in this venue with this type of event, especially if I bring the Rocket with me next time.

The party at the hotel went on until 5am – well, that's the time I departed. I'd like to report exactly what happened, but Mr Carling has somewhat clouded my memories. I do recall everyone having a great time. Lots of laughter, even Fergal smiled. I think Reanne finally got that kiss too.

Before the event I'd had 12 posters mounted up with a commemorative plaque, a limited line of merchandise that we got all the players to sign. Joe Swail kept asking about them, as he wanted one for his snooker room. The truth is they sold out on the first day… all except the one I held back for him.

I presented it to him in the hotel after the event and he was genuinely choked. I got a tricolour flag signed by all the team as well; I gave that to Fergal – a small thank-you for selling a bucketload of tickets.

We were all battered. Dennis confided in me that on Saturday night he had decided to stop playing in these exhibitions as he felt he couldn't do the team justice. He was going to tell me after the event… then near on 800 people cheered and shouted for him, and it reminded him just how much he was loved. 'I'll keep on getting the cue out for as long as you need me, Jason,' he said.

Everyone loves Dennis; I think my girlfriend Michelle loves him more than she does me! Well, I haven't won the world title, have I? He's already getting a new army of fans with his exploits on the new *Real Marigold Hotel*.

The only other people in the bar that night were a wedding party. I think most of their album will end up being photobombed by the players. The bride and groom were deaf, as were most of their guests. As you may know, Joe Swail is partially deaf, and at one point he staggered up and threw his arms round me and Dennis and said, 'They're all deaf! I'm in my fucking element, it's a perfect night!' We all creased up.

Some players had early flights, most never went to bed. It was the perfect ending to the best-ever event I had staged. My only regret was that Michaela wasn't with us.

People talk about the atmosphere in the Crucible.

People talk about the atmosphere in Berlin.

Trust me on this…

There is nothing like the atmosphere created by a full house in Goffs. Absolutely nothing. I love going back.

CHAPTER 32

2016 – A YEAR IN ORBIT WITH A ROCKET

In Cardiff in February 2016, I believe Ronnie played his best snooker since 2012 in capturing his fourth Welsh Open. We had a great week in Wales, just the two of us, sticking to a daily routine which included us popping into the Motorpoint Arena for him to hand out a quick drubbing on the baize to someone before grabbing a Chinese at the Happy Gatherings on Cowbridge Road.

We'd arrived on the back of his fifth Masters title, won at Ally Pally in January with victories over Mark Williams, Mark Selby and Stuart Bingham before a one-sided affair against Barry Hawkins – ironically the player Ronnie was due to face in Sheffield after the Dave Gilbert episode I talked about earlier. Ronnie had passed the 800-century mark against Ricky Walden too and declared he wanted to make 1000.

We'd played loads of exhibitions all over the UK and Europe, from the best club tables with fine match balls to tables that resembled potato fields with a box of avocados to hit round – it was possibly the worst preparation possible for these major events but we'd created some great memories. Ronnie, JV and I, touring the country like a modern-day Travelling Wilburys.

In Wales he immediately hit the ground running, the 4-1 victory over Barry Pinches was not necessarily great snooker, but it contained the now infamous 146 break... The Rocket was making news again!

I was sitting in the players' lounge at the time and from about the eighth or ninth red ball a gathering of players had formed around the sofas with the realisation that the maxi was well on.

There had recently been a lot of debate about the devaluing of the 147 prize. In years gone by you won £147,000 in cash for a maximum.' In many cases that exceeded the tournament winner's cheque.

And then of course, at some events you won a car: the first time it was won it was a particular model from the Eastern bloc and is still fondly remembered by snooker aficionados to this day.

It all happened at the Civic Centre in Oldham in January 1982. A young player called Steve Davis made the first of his many entries into the record books during a frame against John Spencer. It was the Lada Classic tournament, and guess what the prize was for any player who orchestrated the perfect game?

With the match at two all, Spenny broke off and spectated for the next seven minutes as the Nugget rattled in the sprightly maximum, the first time it had been done in a major tournament, and the first time on TV.

Ironically, John Spencer himself had managed a 147 three years earlier in the Holsten International in Slough, but it wasn't ratified. The table he used was found to have pockets that were too big and, worse still, his achievement didn't get captured because the cameramen were off having a tea break!

In 1982 the first televised 147 break was big news; in 1983, when Thorburn did it against Griffiths in Sheffield, it was global news; but by 2016 it had been happening all too often for Barry Hearn, so he downgraded it to a £5,000 rolling prize. As no one had made one at the German Masters in Berlin the prize was 10K in Cardiff – by the time Ronnie got the 14th red, he had already decided it wasn't enough.

The devil took over and he played the penultimate red to land on the pink instead of the black. There was a hushed silence, followed by laughter as he potted it, in doing so sacrificing the 147 prize and ten bags to suit.

The humour – and it seemed almost admiration – that circulated the players' room soon became a divisive conversation point. Barry Hearn issued a statement. He labelled it 'unacceptable and disrespectful' but privately he thought it was hilarious – and don't forget he thought he'd saved himself £8,000, as the high-break prize for the tournament was only £2,000. His hilarity soon vanished when Ding made a 147 in his match with Neil Robertson; Ronnie remarked: 'Ding's let the team down there, I'll have to have a word'.

Only Ronnie would have had the bollocks to do such a thing. It was a protest, but at the same time it was commercial gold for the tournament as the 146 became headlines and highlighted to millions the fact that there was an event actually taking place in Wales that week. It's amazing how so many people still believe snooker is only played three times a year the BBC events and many more think it's only played in Sheffield each April.

The newly crowned OBE was making news again and we were only on Day 1. It wasn't all admiration though, as I said; £10,000 would make a lot of difference to 99 per cent of all snooker fans, including me. And of course he could have gone for the maximum break, possibly made it, and donated it to charity.

The 'charity' criticism is impossible to rebut, but I've gone on record before to state just how much Ronnie and Jimmy donate to charity. I should know as I administer it – and I have had to keep records and receipts of everything we donate and give away to good causes as it was sticking out on my balance sheet. Of course if Ronnie had made the 147, then donated the money to a charity of his choice, it would have been a great gesture, but hindsight is a wonderful thing, and in the moment, in the heat of battle I defy any top sportsman's mind to be wandering away from the competition to decide where he's donating his prize winnings.

The issue was still bubbling away by the time we got to our next match, Tian Pengfei, an experienced player from China. As so often, at the moment he is faced with the most adversity, something in Ronnie's game clicked. It was 4-0 in just over 39 minutes with breaks of 110, 90, 112 and 102. Tian only scored 37 points in the entire match. During my nightly phone call to my partner I told her I was definitely here for the week. I could tell he was hitting the ball really well, the practice table was covered in chalk slugs, a tell-tale sign, in Ronnie's own view, that means he is getting through the ball well. We were going through a whole practice session without him missing a single ball: it was frightening stuff.

The round-three match only took 55 minutes – he was getting slower! A 4-0 win over Jimmy Robertson that included a 94, a 131 and 300 unanswered points. Jimmy Robertson is no mug; he was ranked 34 in the world at the time of the match.

In the last 16 he faced my old friend Yu Delu, the man who could have ruined the first Legends appearance for Stephen Hendry in 2012. Yu is another fine player, the first person to score a 147 on the China Professional Tour, but I knew Ronnie was already looking beyond him and a potential meeting in the quarters with Mark Selby. Players will tell you they take each match at a time, and I think that's true in the main, but if you are in the groove, if it's coming easy, you are looking to go deep in an event and planning your route.

Yu was beaten 4-1. Ronnie knew he was hitting it well, but he also knew that the true test of what shape his game was in was coming up in a head-to-head with the Jester.

Mark Selby is a dominant force on the table; he has been since

2014. He is so far ahead in the rankings he could put his feet up for a year and not get caught, something he almost had to do after dropping a glass door on his toe and almost severing it early in the 2017 season.

But this was to be Ronnie's week. A hugely impressive victory followed over Mark, five frames to one, with a ridiculous 132 break thrown in. I couldn't see anyone stopping him. I've been at enough events to be realistic, I know the fine lines, I know how good the others players can be, but it just felt like we were invincible.

Joe Perry was dispatched 6-3 in the semis and it was to be Neil Robertson, the 'Thunder from Down Under', in the final – a player who'd made 100 century breaks the season before, a record I don't think Ronnie or anyone else will ever beat.

Neil led 3-1 to the interval; Ronnie's only real contribution was a 60 break in frame 3. After the break it went 5-2 to the Aussie and for the first time since we'd crossed the Severn Bridge we were in trouble.

Ronnie won a crucial eighth frame to only trail 5-3; I think Neil knew he deserved better than that score line, it was 6-2, maybe 7-1 all day long.

Scouse John had arrived from Liverpool, a lifelong friend of Ronnie's from when he was based up in Merseyside. John is funny, no actually he is hilarious, but he is also loud. He is a lovable rogue but by his own admission he can be a nuisance. He must own every set of match balls from every final Ronnie has ever won, but he isn't afraid to give it some when he's in the crowd, and at times Ronnie needs that. So when you are next at a match, or even watching on TV, if you hear a loud Scouse accent roaring 'C'mon the Rocket', that'll be Scouse John; he is family. You'll also see him gate-crashing all the official photo shoots at the end and scampering away from the venue with a set of 1g balls under his arm!

Ronnie won all six frames in the evening session, breaks of 57,

78, 67, 70, 61, finishing with a 141 to defeat Neil 9-5. It was his 28th ranking title, and over the whole week in Cardiff he had won 36 of the 47 frames he competed in. There were also ten century breaks and £60,000 for his troubles.

The ranking points for winning meant Ronnie had gate-crashed the Grand Prix line-up due to be played in four weeks' time. The issue we had was that we were already under contract to be in Casablanca at the same time for the first-ever Snooker Legends in North Africa. Not for the first time we had an issue to sort out. That said, there was nothing on the journey home down the M4 that gave me any indication that the biggest crisis of his career was only eight weeks away...

CHAPTER 33

CRISIS PART 2: WORLD CHAMPIONSHIP R1

18th April 2016

RONNIE O'SULLIVAN 10
DAVE GILBERT 7

The route from the stage door at the Crucible to the Hilton Hotel takes just under five minutes and it's usually a ride where we make the plans for dinner – would it be our mate Ayaz's kebab shop, the Wong Ting Chinese or Koko on Ecclesall Road? I knew it was going to be a sandwich from a garage somewhere down the A1 Motorway, but that's all I knew.

Back in our room on the fifth floor, overlooking the River Don, the plan was made. Damien Hirst was with us but had to leave for London; he felt bad but knew Ronnie was in safe hands with me. He reiterated that all of his resources – and trust me he is a man with resources – were available immediately to me for Ronnie should we need them. Antony Genn was also back with us and while I packed up all the gear he was sitting on the bed with Ronnie – who by now had a bath towel full of ice wrapped around his swelling knuckles. I packed everything: sometimes when we have days off in events we take the bare minimum home and keep the hotel rooms on but I had no doubt that the 2016 World Championship was over. Even a fit and healthy Ronnie, firing on all cylinders, couldn't play without his cue or with a broken right hand. He was as far away from being able to compete as he had ever been.

Anxiety and pressure are not something you can physically see; it's completely individual to that person, and just like depression, it's invisible to the eye. I knew there was nothing physically wrong with Ronnie; I'd been chasing him down the towpath each morning desperate to shift some timber. It was the anxiety and pressure of being at the game's most high-profile event, being the game's most high-profile player and carrying the expectations of millions of snooker fans globally who wanted him to secure a sixth world title.

I think I would need to add exhaustion to the diagnosis as well, and in truth I probably played a part in that bit.

I alluded to the fact we'd been clocking up the air miles over the past 12 months, and we had. Alongside his tournaments and sponsor commitments we'd had trips to Denmark, Morocco, Romania, Bulgaria and Ireland. On each trip we'd met great people, on each trip we played to packed houses, on each trip we were getting paid and looked after... but on each trip Ronnie was expected to perform... every night. Everyone wanted a 147; no, in fact everyone expected a 147. The crazy thing was he was delivering night after night. I forget exactly how many centuries we had but we had 147 breaks in Scunthorpe, Newry, Copenhagen and Lowestoft. You almost felt you were letting people down if they didn't get a maxi. The pressure wasn't showing daily, but no doubt based on what had happened in Sheffield, it had been steadily building.

I had cracked earlier in March during a run that had seen us play a Legends night in Bolton with Jimmy, fly to Denmark for two days and then rush back on the Sunday to do a show at the Arches in Coventry. I'd started feeling ill overnight in Copenhagen. We were doing long days and still trying to train in the day as well, and maybe I was guilty of trying to keep up with Ronnie in the gym, or maybe it was just my body gave up two weeks before his – either way, I was fucked. I made the flight back to Manchester where we picked up the car and we dashed to Coventry. I was in a bit of a daze and once again we were under pressure because of a flight delay, so the pedal was to the metal, so to speak.

We made the hotel with about 30 minutes to spare but to my dismay it was one of these new-fangled places that seem to think they can do without humans! We arrived to find ourselves with an iPad to greet us rather than a real person and we were invited to check in via a game of what looked like Tetris.

Back in the hotel and the big three hit me like a sledgehammer: sickness, diarrhoea and headache. I agreed to meet Ronnie in 25 minutes to travel to the venue, but once I lay down I was out like a light and for the one and only time it was the five-time world champion who was banging on my hotel door to depart for work.

I got through the night, god knows how. I sat in the corner sipping water for most of it. Ronnie had to drive back to Essex and I was in no fit state to continue the journey on my own to Ascot, so he kindly put me up. My phone battery had died; I was out of contact with my own partner so she was obviously worried. She eventually got Ronnie's number from someone else and he confirmed I was OK, if not a little pale! On reflection I think it was the first sign that we'd taken on too much.

Back on the A1 heading south to the capital for his medical appointment Ronnie had begun to realise what had just happened. He wanted to disappear, to run away from everything.

Damien had arrived the day before with a box full of homemade brownies – if you pardon the French, they were the bollocks but so rich you could only handle one a day. We'd packed them with the gear and the box was taking a serious denting as the Rocket was taking on a serious sugar rush – he must have had five or six. It was another clear sign that he had cracked, stopped caring about himself or his body. For someone like me five or six brownies would be a sin, but how can I put it, it wasn't territory I hadn't trodden many times before, but for him, ferociously strict about what he eats, this was another sign of his mental state. In the words of Dr Steve Peters, 'the chimp was running amok'.

By the time we'd hit Luton he'd slept for a bit, I'd changed the ice in the towel at a service station but his fist was still really swollen and a weird purple colour. I'd been given an address to head for. The doctor agreed to treat Ronnie on the grounds of anxiety and exhaustion.

It was late on the Monday, the World Championship was going on in Sheffield but its main attraction was in the care of a doctor.

The world wanted to know where he was, but only a few people knew the truth. It felt good to pass on the responsibility of his wellbeing to someone else; this day had certainly not been part of the original job description.

I woke on Tuesday knowing that I had to prepare for every eventuality. My phone was ringing off the hook and the first headlines had appeared in the tabloids about an incident in Ronnie's dressing room. *The Sun* said he'd been heard smashing up the dressing room. I was named as well.

I glanced over to the corner of my office. Ronnie's case looked like it always did, single, black leather, the 'P' missing from the maker's name meaning it said 'arris'. Aside from that it was in perfect working order; sadly I knew its contents told a different story. I'd not looked at the cue since I packed it away, we'd certainly not discussed it on our trip south – it was only then when I had nothing to do but remain quiet that it dawned on me what was going to happen if Ronnie recovered and decided to play his second-round match on the Saturday. It was ludicrous to even contemplate it but I knew it was my job to try to get his cue fixed... just in case. I got on the phone to John Parris and what followed was a series of clandestine visits to his workshop in Forest Hill where John worked round the clock to repair – no actually rebuild – Ronnie's cue. I cannot give John enough credit for what he did and also how he kept what he was doing quiet – a true professional who deserves all the accolades he gets. I think his equipment has won more world titles in the modern day than any other cue-maker.

By Thursday it was apparent Ronnie was improving. He was beginning to consider the impossible, a return to continue his participation in the World Snooker Championship. I'd learned that he'd only receive a warning for missing the press conference; that was a relief and I also knew, all being well, the cue would be ready for Friday evening.

I'd been driving Ronnie's car round all week; for once my choice of 'whip' fitted in down Ascot high street. It had one final journey to make to John Parris and then one early on Saturday morning to Sheffield – he was making the trip.

His mum dropped off his shoes and suit, and I got him a train ticket.

Whatever happened in those four days, he was totally transformed. The fella who stepped off the East Midlands train service from Euston seemed coherent, bright and had even squeezed in a haircut, which probably made his transformation more dramatic. It had been in its wild and unkempt state during the Gilbert match.

Damien was back in town and I think he too was startled at just how well rested Ronnie looked – the glint was back in his eye. His knuckles meant he'd be shaking hands left-handed for a bit, but he could hold a cue and that meant he could compete.

History will show that we came up a little bit short; although he lost 13-12 to Barry Hawkins the stats will show he lost every single scrappy close frame, winning his 12 mostly in single visits. I think in hindsight the toll of the week had to have been a factor in a 25-frame match under the scrutiny and intensity. This time he did the press conference and he alluded a bit to the issues of the week, but it was only a very truncated and largely vague statement.

That week showed me that as important as winning the World Championship was, it wasn't worth having a breakdown for. When people ask why people like Ronnie get the big bucks I always wonder whether they would have the courage to take themselves right to the edge of sanity – because I truly believe sometimes that's what it takes to scale the heights he reaches.

Mark Selby was a deserving winner in Sheffield that year, but I actually think the challenge Ronnie faced during those two weeks, and the depths to which he dropped only to then drag himself up again made him a winner, too.

I believe what he learned during that tournament has probably prolonged his career for another ten years. Changes needed to be made.

CHAPTER 34

CAR SHARE: THE ELEVEN-30 SERIES

I blame myself for some of Ronnie's problems during 2016. We'd been greedy and tried to work full-time on the exhibition circuit and also participate full-time in professional events. *Peter Kay's Car Share* is a British sitcom set around a supermarket manager (Peter Kay) and promotions rep Kayleigh Kitson and their participation in a company car-sharing scheme. They form an unlikely bond from hours of sitting together in traffic – it felt at times during that year Ronnie and I were making a spin-off of the show, although fair to say the Audi RS4 and Porsche were slightly better transport than the Fiat Kay drove.

Of course, as was so often the case, when I'd booked the exhibitions and we took up fantastic opportunities to visit places like Casablanca and Copenhagen, the intention was not to participate in the World Snooker events. The lure of titles, ranking points, and professional competition was too much for Ronnie to ignore. So he has to take a lot of responsibility for our schedule too, I guess.

We both knew after the issues in Sheffield that we had to

start looking after ourselves and take the foot off the gas. Being away so much was good for the bank balance but not so good for the balance of life. I wanted to earn but I also wanted to see my partner; it wasn't doing either of us any good with me being away for so long.

I'd already got on top of some of the chaos, very gradually getting Ronnie's life off the table in order. Previous bad management had meant things had been missed: it was like a million-piece jigsaw puzzle titled 'Headache'. On top of that he had a court case going on. Just as in Sheffield, I stood by him every step of the way in what was a horribly stressful situation, motivated and initiated for the wrong reasons. The outcome was the same, save the fortune Ronnie spent on lawyers' fees.

Amongst the exhibitions, where he played club players or sponsors, we'd decided to set up a series of challenge matches, something to give Ronnie some hard match practice on match tables. The Eleven-30 Series was created, and Judd Trump was signed up for a series of six shows with a £30,000 winner-takes-all prize put up by our sponsor Dafabet. We also got the players some appearance money but the pot was real and there to be won!

The idea was to get a bit rock and roll, try to create an atmosphere that people could enjoy, loud music between frames, flashing lights and quick-fire attacking snooker. Players bought into the idea; I think Judd found the hospitality hard but it was clear that rather than being rivals the players actually enjoyed each other's company. I could have done with a bit more trash talk to spice it up.

Jimmy was involved as well, playing a token frame at the end of the night for a raffle winner, and it was good to be able to use some of the sponsor's money to give him six nights' work. We played a famous darts venue to open the series, the Lakeside Country Club in Surrey. Judd won that night but it was clear the audience were struggling to let go; the traditionalists didn't quite know how to behave. It went OK but I had my doubts as to whether anything could really break the muted traditions of a game spanning back to 1875. It certainly wasn't going to happen overnight.

I did a lot of social media before we arrived in Belfast to try to tell people it was OK to get involved. It would be the biggest audience of the tour, over 2,000 in, and there was definitely a more relaxed atmosphere to it. The only thing was that Judd won again, and of course the audience was heavily biased towards the Rocket. With Ronnie 2-0 down, the visit to Kildare for leg three took on a whole new level of importance. I've waxed lyrical enough about Goffs but of course it was rammed again, and the Rocket rose to the occasion and the majority of the paddies left happy. For the Eleven-30 Series... it was game on!

Lord Russell Baker and his Amber Dew Events company was our next host. We'd sold the show in, so no risk to me financially, but this fellow knew what he was doing: it sold out easily. It was a local gig, Peterborough, and a tale of two car journeys. Ronnie had just taken delivery of a new grey 911 Porsche and he decided to drive us up the M11 and stretch its legs. It was quick and we nearly lost it on a roundabout where the road was a bit damp. If I had been driving then we'd have been in the hedge; Ronnie is an experienced track driver. Then again, if I'd been driving we wouldn't have been trying to straight-line the roundabout in the first place.

Judd's journey didn't quite go as well as ours. DJango, his manager, was also stretching the legs of his German sports car and he picked up an unwelcome passenger in the form of a six-inch nail at about 70 miles an hour! They made it to the hard shoulder but they were stranded, and a little shaken. Judd had to call for a rescue and when his mate duly arrived at the venue, having picked him up, with little more than ten minutes to spare it was clear his preparation for leg four had been far from ideal.

Ronnie battered him 6-0 in about 90 minutes. Thank goodness we had Jimmy in the line-up to stretch out the night otherwise

Lord Baker's audience could have been home for the second part of *Corrie*. They'd seen a ruthless display from the Rocket, so I am not aware that anyone complained, but it did feel weird to be leaving the theatre by 9pm. So, two each in the series and we travelled to Bradford for a night where we finally got our rock-and-roll atmosphere, coupled with plenty of unruly Yorkshire behaviour.

My good friend Mick was staging the event; we opened the doors at 3pm for a Jimmy exhibition, with the main event a good four hours and by average six beers per person away. It was great for a cut of the bar sales we were on, not so great for the state of the audience! Over 1,400 were packed into the arena by the time Ronnie and Judd walked out. The noise was deafening and it did feel a bit like two boxers going into battle. It was hard to keep a clear access route and the back slaps and outstretched hands got right on their nerves. Ronnie won but I'm not really sure how many people were that bothered – they'd seen the players, filled up on the cheap beer and were off en masse to the casino to see Kell Brook get his face rearranged by Gennady Golovkin.

With Ronnie having won three on the trot, it was Judd who needed to win the final in Preston and make at least three centuries to take the prize; it was a big ask. The Guild Hall is an iconic snooker venue but with World Snooker taking the qualifiers there, and people being able to see all players, including Ros and Trump, for a fiver, there is no doubt it cannibalised our sales.

It wasn't really the finale I wanted, a bit of a damp squib really. The table seemed to play hard and although Judd won to make the series three all, he never got close to getting past the centuries made by Ronnie. Honours even in the series.

It is generally accepted in the world of snooker that if Ronnie plays to his best then he will win the majority of competitions he enters, especially when matches are contested over the longer format.

You would think that all his challengers would be looking to see what Ronnie does that gives him that 'edge'. It's not about potting balls: all professionals, and many top amateur and club players, can clear a snooker table and – let's face it – snooker is still an individual sport. It's you against the table.

As far as I am aware, in over a hundred years, the positions of the pockets have never moved, and it's still a bit of wood you hold, with a lump of leather on the end of it. I will concede the balls are no longer ivory, but my point is the game hasn't changed. In tennis, for example, how the ball gets hit back across the net from your opponent can influence how you play. In snooker, it's you and the table; Ronnie can't make you miss from sitting in his chair.

Ronnie is an elite sportsman. He eats the right things, he trains in the gym and yet even though none of these traits are hidden, it seems unbelievable that none of the other top players try to copy him.

Rory McIlroy said that when he started playing golf he wanted to know everything about Tiger Woods, from his course management right down to what he had for breakfast, when he ate it and which sort of spoon he would use.

I was with Ronnie at the Champion of Champions in 2014 when he played Marco Fu. At the interval, 4-0 up, Ronnie was tucking into fresh smoked salmon with lemon juice; he made sure he got half a litre of water through him during that 15 minutes to rehydrate, then topped up on nuts and enjoyed a nice cup of tea chatting to me about how his concentration was. This wasn't him relaxing; this was his match preparation for the second half.

Marco was sat alone in the tournament office. Madness to me that in a tournament carrying a first prize of £100,000, he didn't have some sort of support network with him. He needed someone there to remind him how bloody good a player he is.

I've seen so many players treat the mid-sessions as a time to get on their phones, eat a chocolate bar, grab a cigarette or do their social media. Seriously, do you see Roger Federer tweeting between the change of ends, or Lionel Messi posting up a selfie at half-time?

Then of course there is the way Ronnie has embraced the mental aspect of the game and his association with Dr Steve Peters.

To my knowledge Steve Peters can't make a 20 break; he has no concept of what a snooker stance or a cue action is, or knows what type of tip Ronnie uses, but you ask the Rocket what the most important aspect was of his remarkable win at the World's in 2013 and he will repeatedly refer to the mental coaching of his doctor.

Why aren't all the other top players knocking on Steve's door? Why don't they see the way the best player in the world lives his life and try to learn from it? Is it because they are happy with mediocrity? Or are they just too lazy?

There is generally only one first place. I guess it all comes down to how much you are willing to sacrifice to get a shot at it.

For the time being it's pretty difficult to shoot higher than a Rocket, even though for those 12 months we did all we could with our heavy workload to make it misfire.

CHAPTER 35

BEIJING 9-BALL

It was just an ordinary game of 9-Ball, nothing like the £15,000 money matches that happen at my club in Newbury on a regular basis, but in some ways this 'set' was far more important that any cue sports match I'd ever been associated with.

My opponent was Barry Hearn and the setting was the Leaguen club in Beijing; the local time was 2am, the month November, the year 2017 and the libation of choice was Chinese tea rather than the 1982 Château Lafite Rothschild we'd been consuming earlier in the evening.

I won 5-4, largely irrelevant in 9-Ball history, but any victory over Mr Hearn deserves documenting. Fair to say neither of us was going to trouble the Mosconi Cup selectors, but it was during this 'bash around' that I got the green light to take over the World Seniors Championship, and more importantly I got a place at Ponds Forge in Barry's World Professional Championship for my winner.

For some time Jason Ferguson had been telling me that he always thought I'd have a part to play in the Seniors game, but as flattering as that was, I knew nothing would come from his support without approval, and sign off, from the main man.

I guess it's almost ironic that the key moment in what I hope will become my legacy in the game happened on a freezing cold November night in a city formerly known as Old Peking, somewhere I'd been many times in my former pantomime life with Widow Twankey and Abanazar. I felt like it was me who got to rub the magic lamp rather than Aladdin that night, and Barry Hearn was my genie!

We were all on our way back from the snooker International Championship in Daqing. The city is two hours north of Beijing and known as the oil capital of China. A local billionaire, and snooker fan, Mr Ju bumped into the chairman of the WPBSA in a downtown 'Hot Pot' and decided he wanted to stage a snooker event in his home town. To give you some geography, Daqing sits in the Heilongjiang province – the name literally means 'Great celebration', which is an emotion you must feel constantly in this place if you have a winter coat or heating business, because it was minus 30 at times ('brass monkeys' as my fiancée's northern parents say). A hundred miles to the north and you're in Siberia, the same west and you'll end up in Mongolia, and if you're after a little weekend break then you'll find Pyongyang and Kim Jong-un only a couple of hours away to the east.

I'd been part of a deal which guaranteed Ronnie's participation in the International Championship; it was a deal set up for travelling to China to play in the tournament, but also for some PR activities. Ronnie had to promote the tournament and attend and publicise a foundation in the name of the mother of China, Soong Ching-ling. It wasn't all meetings and dinners though – we also visited a school that houses children who have been orphaned from Tibet. It was very humbling and moved many of us to tears.

Mr Ju, like so many other billionaires in China, is encouraged to invest some of his business profits into good causes. When Xi

Jinping became the General Secretary of the Communist Party of China, in effect the leader, he made a point of saying he wanted to get the Chinese people more active, which roughly translated means: 'I want to see you all invest in sport, or all the billions you lot are making from government contracts will soon dry up.' There is no doubt that the dramatic rise in the popularity of football in China has been driven by this mandate.

The Chinese Super League, CSL, has seen an investment to date of 4.8 billion dollars; that's more than our own Premier League over the same period. Places like China and North America were once seen as places where 'legends' of the sport went to play their last couple of seasons at a gentler pace. It was, in effect, an extended testimonial. Now you have many more current football players heading to the CSL. Former Manchester City player, Carlos Tevez, reportedly picks up a cool £634,000 a week with Shanghai Shenhua, but even he is playing second fiddle to Lavezzi at Hebei China Fortune, who has to make do with just £798,000 a week. And they say snooker players get paid too much!

Having spent a week doing this promotional work in Beijing before heading north to actually play some snooker, it was clear that everything in China is about government. No matter how much money or power you think you have, if you haven't got the government onside, you can forget it. I sat at a dinner with a certain mayor of a major city who proclaimed to a large table of dignitaries, which included Barry and Ronnie, that China would stage the World Cup by 2034 – and it would win it.

The impact from China on our sport has been huge; it's so important it had seen Barry find the time to come to Beijing to not just play 9-Ball with me but to discuss future plans, and investment, in tournaments. Mr Ju wanted to spend his money and Barry wanted to make sure some of it was floating in his direction.

The World Seniors Snooker Championship was first held in 1991 with 16 players all aged over 40. It took place at the Trentham Gardens in Stoke and was promoted by Matchroom, Barry's company. The final was contested between the two highest-ranked players, with Cliff Wilson defeating Eddie Charlton 5-4 to become the inaugural champion. The event was revived in 2010 by Joe Johnson and Dave Shipley, but the field was reduced to nine players and was played in Bradford. I attended it and saw Jimmy White become the champion. It was a great night and was run in exactly the same atmosphere as our Legends nights – relaxed, with humour, but still competitive.

In 2011 the age was increased to 45 years, and it was moved to Peterborough. All matches were best of three, a 30-second shot clock was introduced after ten minutes of play, and the miss rule was altered so ball-in-hand was awarded anywhere on table after the third miss. For the record, I've never been a fan of that one and it's not used in my events. The field was increased to 16 players, with 12 being invited and the other four coming through qualifying. Amateur Darren Morgan from Wales won the event.

By 2015 the event had returned to an over 40 year age limit, all former World Seniors Champions and World Snooker Champions who registered for the event were seeded through to Blackpool, and the remaining places were filled through a qualifying event. More importantly, then current tour professionals over 40 were allowed to play in it; it was the final tinkering in an attempt for Sky TV and World Snooker to make it a viable event. I think Barry would admit it backfired, as no one truly believed that top-16 players like Mark Williams, who unbelievably was 39 when he played in it, could be beaten by a 69-year-old Cliff Thorburn. People switched off and Barry dropped the event completely.

My idea was to take a lot of what we'd already created with the Snooker Legends but also to learn from what Joe and Dave had done in 2010. In some ways, if they had been allowed to continue with the project, the opportunity I now had might not have been there. The numbers weren't big enough for Barry and so he lost interest.

My project, exciting as it was to me, and as well supported as it seemed by Mr Hearn, had one major problem that neither of us could solve – the fourth dimension: Time.

On paper I was going to re-launch the World Seniors Snooker Championship, on paper I was going to give opportunities for any amateur player globally to win a qualifier, win the event and take their place in Sheffield... However, on paper it was already the end of November and all the qualifiers and the main event itself had to be done and dusted by the start of April as that's when the players ranked 17-128, and my champion, would begin their qualification for the Crucible at Ponds Forge.

I'm well known for loving a challenge, but this one was going to be tough for me. I had no venue, no qualifiers booked and no tournament entry system, let alone any terms for participation.

I needed something to spark this; I needed something that would get people talking and make this more than just another tournament for the old boys...

I needed the King of the Crucible.

CHAPTER 36

DARING TO DREAM: HENDRY'S COMEBACK

Fego's in Ascot isn't cheap: it charges £4 for a coffee and £8 for poached eggs with something that resembles a hedgerow grab thrown on top. It's somewhere my partner and I go on special occasions for brunch, but today was a different sort of special occasion as I was going to try to pitch my vision for the World Seniors Snooker Championship to Stephen Hendry.

I felt that if this project was going to be viable I needed the King of the Crucible to come on board and make a competitive comeback. Moreover, its was almost 2017, I needed people to believe he could win it and once more play in the world professional championships. That was the 'big story' the idea of me taking on the World Seniors could slipstream and benefit from.

My gut feeling told me he was looking for a reason to play again but that I was going to have to give him a very good reason to get him back to the practice table for an event in which he felt he could do himself justice.

His initial reaction was lukewarm, at best. He knew I could put on a good event, but the chance I was offering for him to co-promote it with me didn't seem to interest him greatly. In hindsight I'm not sure why I was surprised: snooker players play snooker, they are successful because they are selfish and ruthless and operate alone. Trying to entice them with spreadsheets and business plans is really a waste of time

I left with an agreement to run the idea past his new agent. I'd always worked direct with Stephen before, as I do with many of the players, but I'm not averse to an agent, providing they are acting in everyone's long-term interests and not looking for a quick smash and grab. Thankfully, Stephen's agent, Jane, did see the value in what I was suggesting and thought it was a perfect vehicle for Stephen to start playing some snooker again. I think it was clear to her, and her team, that Stephen Hendry playing snooker was far more valuable than Stephen Hendry playing Chinese Pool or doing things like cooking on *MasterChef* or sitting in *Big Brother*. He was in and we'd announce it when he was on-air at the Masters, BBC promotion never a bad thing!

I'd love to say I enjoyed the festivities that Christmas, but the truth was I was already under pressure, pinning everything on the announcement that would come at Ally Pally. I'd hoped to be able to use the World Snooker tournament entry system – it's fully automated, secure and allows access globally... It wasn't available to me, and this was going to be a cost I hadn't budgeted for.

I've been really lucky to have the same IT guy since 1997. Like me, a former children's entertainer, Rob at RNG took an interest in computers in the early days and carved himself a career for when the inevitable happened and people no longer wanted men in loud trousers and shirts making balloon dogs in their front rooms while their kids were being traumatised by Judy beating the hell out of Mr Punch.

He worked non-stop to build me a system to handle entries for the four qualifiers for which I'd found free weekends. I was lucky to be able to make my own club available in Newbury but I also had contacts in Leeds, a good friend and promoter in Nuremberg, Germany, and Ken Doherty found me a club in Dublin – we were international, well at least European!

Over the years I've worked in almost every theatre in the UK, it's been with some of the best theatre mangers – people with vision, drive and flexibility. I've also worked with some of the worst. I didn't choose Scunthorpe as the host town for the World Seniors Championship; I chose the theatre's manager, Dan Harris. I knew Dan could get his end sorted quickly, and efficiently, and that he would motivate his whole team at the Baths Hall to get this thing on sale, promoted and performed. It was certainly one of my better decisions, as he came up trumps and we found a gem of a theatre, newly refurbished and with fantastic facilities.

Entries started flooding in for the qualifiers, Hazel Irvine had done me a right turn in giving it a plug on the BBC, and Stephen and JP had commented live on-air on how great the idea was.

The dream of an amateur player winning a qualifier, beating Hendry to win the World Seniors Championship, winning seven more matches in Sheffield and defeating Ronnie on the final black on a bank holiday Monday to become World Professional Snooker Champion was now possible. Perhaps it was far-fetched, but with what I'd created the important thing was it could happen, and a bloke in darts called Rob Cross created a similar fairy-tale story in becoming Darts World Champion from amateur spear-chucker in under a year. I came up with the hashtag #daretodream and it stuck and has become more relevant than I ever imagined.

As some familiar names registered, I had to check they were not still professional players who had entered by mistake, not understanding the rules. Barry Pinches, Gerard Greene and our eventual winner Peter Lines were all players I assumed still had a tour card. I was wrong and was immediately struck by how tasty the standard of these qualifiers was going to be.

Also littered amongst the field were an army of former players who wouldn't be household names to many but were once holders of tour cards. Entries were received from the likes of Filtness, Richardson, Lanigan, Parnell and one I did know, Les Dodd, the 1987 English Professional Snooker Runner Up. Les was exactly the type of player this tour was made for, a good old former-pro who'd become better known for putting on Ronnie's tips than playing the game himself.

From early on, Peter Lines from Leeds was everyone's hot favourite, but club tables can be a leveller, as could the format I'd adopted for these events: the black ball re-spot. Nothing I have done has divided opinion more than the black-ball decider at two frames all. Some players love them, many hate them, but everyone agrees they add drama and that's what I, with an entertainment background, crave. Trust me, no one gathers round a table watching two people slug out a fifth frame, but you do see them glued to the re-spot decider.

There's a fine line between a glorious victory and a complete twitch-up, but I will always argue it's those fine moments that define many of the greatest moments in sport, not just snooker. You can technically coach anyone, but you cannot coach bottle, and all great champions and winners have it in abundance.

When James Farrell doubled the re-spot into the middle bag at about 100 mph from the break-off in Cookstown, the footage online made him an internet sensation. Ask *him* how he feels about the re-spot!

Historically the World Seniors matches were played over a best of three frames; my format was already giving them four frames, more bang for their buck, but if it went to two all then we were going to settle it on the black – still a legitimate rule in our game if scores are tied at the end of a frame. There is no fancy manipulation of what the man who created the game of snooker,

Sir Neville Francis Fitzgerald Chamberlain, played in 1875 in what I am doing, but there is guaranteed drama.

By the time we got to Scunthorpe we had our four qualifiers, those who would dare to dream. Peter Lines had made it as predicted, but so had another former professional, Patrick Wallace from Northern Ireland. The other two qualifiers were not so well known, Jonathan Bagley was a taxi driver from Leeds, and Aidan Owens was a snooker-club owner from Lowestoft.

When the draw came out, Aidan got Willie Thorne, another legend I'd persuaded to play once more. Willie had gone public on his eyesight issues; he had no expectations... Owens was already looking beyond him and a match-up with Hendry. I'd not seen that kind of confidence in a player since Tony Knowles played Davis in 1982. Aidan was dreaming big, and I loved it!

CHAPTER 37

THE 2017 WORLD SENIORS CHAMPIONSHIP

By the time we got to the final of the 2017 World Seniors Championship it already had a Wikipedia page. It was incredible how quickly this idea was growing.

Our eight legends and four qualifiers descended on the Forest Pines Hotel & Golf Resort in Scunthorpe, with the main focus of the media around the competitive comeback of a certain Stephen Hendry.

We'd seeded the top four and drawn our four qualifiers into matches with seeds five to eight. There had been some grumbling about how we had set up our seeding, particularly from one former World Seniors Champion, but I'd already been aware this could occur and had worked with the WPBSA on a legends list based on previous achievements in the game. I wanted to be able to answer any criticism of the chosen eight seeds for the finals stages.

Qualifying players were ranked in order of:

1) Most world titles won
2) Most triple crown events won
3) Most ranking events won
4) Most total professional tournaments won (ranking or invitational)
5) Highest world ranking.

For the purposes of this list, all UK Championship titles would be classed as full-ranking event wins, including those during its period as a non-ranking event.

The top eight were Hendry, Davis, Reardon, Thorburn, Taylor, Parrott, Johnson, Griffiths and Mountjoy. As predicted, Reardon and Mountjoy declined: Ray felt he was too old and Doug was suffering ill health and had in effect 'retired' after we gave him a return to the Crucible in 2016. Steve Davis made it clear he was supportive of my idea but in his email to me he said he had no desire to play competitive snooker any more. I was disappointed to be honest, as he adds huge value to any event he is associated with, but I had to accept his decision.

That meant I was left with the following roll of honour:

Stephen Hendry – 7 World titles, 18 Triple Crown events.
Cliff Thorburn – 1 World title, 4 Triple Crown events.
John Parrott – 1 World title, 2 Triple Crown events,
    9 ranking events.
Dennis Taylor – 1 World title, 2 Triple Crown events,
    2 ranking events.
Joe Johnson – 1 World title, 1 Triple Crown events.
Patsy Fagan – 0 World titles, 1 Triple Crown events.
Tony Knowles – 0 World titles, 0 Triple Crown events,
    2 ranking events.

Tony Meo – 0 World titles, 0 Triple Crown events,
1 ranking event, 8 professional events.

I knew seven of those would be in but that Tony Meo would be a challenge. I've never really got the full story about why he walked away from snooker. I don't know him personally enough to hear it first-hand but I've heard bits and pieces. Either way it's a shame he isn't involved in a game he gave so much to. Tony was polite, but declined, and so I turned to the great WT.

Mr Maximum, Willie Thorne, is one of snooker's biggest names despite only ever winning one ranking event, The Mercantile Classic in 1984. There's no doubt he should have been UK Champion in 1985 – he led Davis 13-10 at the start of the evening session, only to miss a simple blue off its spot and lose 16-14. A few of the boys remind him of that from time to time!

He's had his problems off the table, health and monetary. I've used him a couple of times as an MC but he will always be third on that list; to get more work I needed Willie Thorne to do what he used to do… pot balls. It was touch and go. Try as he might he just could not get his glasses right to play, but we got him to Scunthorpe to give it a go.

He got a stinker of a draw: he was going to be in Aidan Owens' path to get to Hendry. Then again, all four qualifiers were here to win and history shows one of them did.

The unlikely hero from round one was Bradford's Joe Johnson. He was the only seed to win, and he did it in style, a 3-0 victory over Northern Ireland's Patrick Wallace. He instantly gave my event credibility and validity; I'd heard a few comments before about these legends being wheeled out to sell a few tickets but with no chance of making any progress, apart from Hendry who apparently only had to turn up to win it.

The casualties from my legends pool were Patsy Fagan, beaten 3-0 by Peter Lines, Willie, who despite winning his first frame in 17 years, lost out 3-1 to Aidan, and a gallant Tony Knowles who went down on a black ball re-spot to Jonathan Bagley. I didn't know then that Bagley would dominate the first year of the World Seniors Tour, remaining undefeated in all qualifiers in 2017.

The big guns joined on Day 2 and it was drama from the off: the King of the Crucible was returning.

A contractual engagement in China had left Hendry far short of where he wanted to be and it took a dramatic re-spotted black for him to end the dreams of Aidan Owens from Lowestoft. Peter Lines dispatched Dennis 3-0, and Bagley and Parrott did the same to Thorburn and Johnson respectively.

I had Leo Scullion on board, another addition to the Legends family, and a more charming gentleman you couldn't wish to meet, along with Michaela. In many respects he was the senior referee on site.

The big match attracted almost 1.5 million in China, all hoping that Hendry could find a way back to the Crucible in Sheffield. Sadly, as is so often the way in sport, the reality was Peter Lines was just off-tour, much sharper and used to the conditions of a match table. He ran out a comfortable 3-0 winner.

The second semi-final was much closer; in fact it got decided on a black ball re-spot. John Parrott knocked out the taxi driver, who had battled admirably on his first venture into the big time.

The final was a bit of a non-event, Peter Lines running out a 4-0 winner and lifting the title of World Seniors Snooker Champion. In addition to the winner's cheque, Lines received a place in the qualifying tournament for the 2017 World Professional Snooker Championship in Sheffield.

He won the 2017 tournament without losing a single frame, receiving £10,000. He would go on to win a qualifying round at Ponds Forge, another £8,000, and he won his professional tour card back. It was a pretty good month for him; it was a significant one for me. The dream of a sustainable World Seniors Snooker Tour was getting closer.

CHAPTER 38

A NEW WORLD SENIORS TOUR

As soon as the 2017 World Senior Championship was over, I was weighing up whether I could make a full tour out of what I'd started. What I knew couldn't happen was for me to carry on looking after Ronnie full-time and while also trying to build a full-time Seniors Tour. Working with the Rocket and doing some Snooker Legends shows was guaranteed money; this was going to be a risk and I'd have to sacrifice a lot of what was giving me my income. Sleepless nights.com

After he lost to Mark Selby in York for the 2016 UK Championship, I'd talked with Ronnie about securing my services full-time, I would have stopped all Legends exhibitions, my work with ROK Mobile, my seniors' events, and devoted myself purely to his day-to-day management for a guaranteed salary. He didn't want to pay what I wanted, fair enough, but he didn't want to lose me either. We tried a salary for three months but then he got cold feet, worried that having an employee gave me rights if things went wrong. He didn't want the responsibility of having someone working for him, so it went back to being a consultancy relationship.

Something had to change: since September 2016 I'd done three trips to China, excursions to Romania, Germany and Bulgaria, and spent countless nights in UK hotel rooms. I hadn't been home and as far as I was concerned what I was getting paid wasn't enough for what was expected of me. I'd attended important meetings on his behalf; some related to playing but others to legal matters with his ex, all out of my personal time. I was caught trying to juggle lots of roles, and probably not doing any of them that well. And, truthfully, I was enjoying the Seniors' role the best; amateur players were so complimentary about what I was trying to do. I can't blame Ronnie for the situation we were in, it just kind of snow-balled with never a good time to stop and reflect what was going on.

Ronnie and I agreed to more of a part-time role, something to allow me to continue doing my work, and the agent who had only handled his non-snooker deals to date was now tasked with covering all of the deals. I quickly realised it was impossible to look after Ronnie part-time, especially when the agent needed to learn about snooker and I had to be the conduit. Once again I was providing an out-of-hours 24/7 service for Ronnie but being paid for a part-time role. It came to a head again after he won the UK in 2017, and with my deal in place with Jason and Barry, I knew in my heart where I wanted to be but I also felt too much loyalty to simply walk away from the Rocket.

We tried to negotiate a basic fee for what I was currently doing day-to-day, with options for days at tournaments and our exhibitions. Ronnie and I couldn't agree a fee that we both felt comfortable with, so on the trip home after he lost to Mark Allen at the Masters we basically agreed to stop any day-to-day management and remain friends doing our exhibitions. On the whole it's easier for everyone, and certainly my relationship with the WPBSA, if I'm not the spokesman for the game's most controversial player who doesn't always see eye to eye with the people running his sport.

For the first season of the World Seniors Tour I'd decided on four main events, and an ambitious 16 qualifiers. We made entrance fees cheaper, agreed one for China, and also came close to delivering one in New York City. We still had our place in the World Championship for our winner but I started leaning on the WPBSA for more opportunities for our champions.

I had Scunthorpe sorted for the World's and I knew I could use Goffs and simply change the event from Irish Legends Cup to the Senior Irish Masters; now I needed to land the big one – a World Seniors Tour event in the Crucible.

The thought of being able to use my usual one-night exhibition date to stage my Masters event really got my juices flowing. Just like any footballer growing up dreams of playing at Wembley, so any snooker player would love to play in the Crucible. It was ambitious and not easy to deliver, especially as the lady who had been my contact there for eight years had left her job.

As with so many things I do, I simply announced it was happening and then worked on making it viable. It was in the World Seniors' Calendar and I didn't even have a contract to produce my one-night exhibition, let alone two sessions and a competitive event. It was brave but I knew we needed it. I sold the new programmer my dream and made it happen. The format needed to be shortened but I made sure two amateur snooker players would get that chance to walk out and play a legend in the Crucible. Another lifetime memory assured for two more people down to Snooker Legends.

I needed a Southern venue; I was getting criticism, like World Snooker do, of having too many tournaments in the North. It's no accident that the only major snooker event in London is the Masters, and that's the furthest south they go. Northern venues are cheaper, usually have better logistics such as parking and access, and in my experience you get a different breed of people who really want to get on board and make it a success. And that's a compliment coming from someone born as far away from the North as is geographically possible in the UK!

I had done well in Redhill in the past. As I wrote earlier, it was a place where the first-ever 147 in Legends history was made, it was a theatre close to my heart having performed there more than 100 times, and it was in Surrey. But the theatre had a new manager and as soon as I agreed and published the date I knew I'd made a mistake. 'Sorry that's not possible' or 'We can't do that' are two phrases I would never get from Dan in Scunthorpe; I was getting it all the time while planning for the UK Seniors Championship. Then we had parking issues, even problems doing a simple group email.

The only positives from the event itself were the matches themselves, and the fact Jimmy White secured a title and shared it with his teenage son Tommy. Both people had tears in their eyes afterwards; Jimmy's were of joy, mine of frustration. It was only my TV deal with China that got me out of trouble.

Four weeks before the UK Champs, I'd done enough to finally get round a table with Barry Hearn and Jason Ferguson. Jason had seen enough to realise I had something worth getting involved with, and the fact Barry gave up his time to meet us meant he must have seen it too. He arrived with a deal in mind and we'd shaken hands in less than five minutes. It was a great deal for everyone: it gave me accreditation and protection but it also meant I couldn't cannibalise any of Barry's broadcast partners if, for example, a certain high-profile player, who was over 40, decided to retire and move over to the World Seniors Tour.

We got an agreement for the permanent inclusion of all current and future invitational wildcard holders and a promise to help find opportunities. Not everything will kick in until the 2018/19 season, and of course for me the change is working with committees rather than solo. I understand the need to be cautious; in effect the WPBSA has committed itself to a World

Seniors Tour – what happens if I decide next year I don't want to do it any more? Then they are left with a huge albatross and an amateur World Ranking List with more than 200 players to service. If they were inside my head they'd know that's not going to happen but at the same time, if we can grow this, and then someone comes along who can take the tour to the next level and acquire my shares, then I also won't stand in the way.

Steve Davis winning the Alex Higgins Trophy in Goffs was special, especially as Lauren Higgins presented it to him. I'll argue it was his ninth Irish Masters title. For now, people will probably say it won't count, but if I have my way and this World Seniors Tour really takes off then it will do soon.

In March 2018 the dream I had of an unknown amateur player becoming World Seniors Snooker Champion happened. Aaron Canavan, a car valeter from Jersey, defeated Patrick Wallace on a sudden death black ball to write his name forever in snooker cue sports history. A journey he started in Dunstable, winning a qualifier, will take him to Sheffield in April 2018 to play in the World Professional Championship. He is living the dream, he is proof that it can happen.

CHAPTER 39

THE FUTURE

I understand things won't always go right and I won't always make good decisions. I can be guilty of letting my heart rule my head; no one dares to dream more than me. I'm not afraid to try to make a difference but I always like to try to see the best in people. Sometimes I get it very wrong but I'm a huge believer in karma.

In 2013 I became involved in a deal for a snooker cue alongside a coach who wanted to be a businessman. It was without doubt the worst decision in snooker I have ever made.

I still have my involvement with Reanne Evans – being there when she beat Robin Hull in the first round of the 2017 World Professional Snooker Championship ranks as one of my best moments in snooker. If I ever had a sister, I'd want her to be like Reanne: she asks for nothing and works hard for what she achieves. I don't think in my lifetime you'll see a better ladies' snooker player. How she has not been given an MBE is beyond me, but it's something I've been working on behind the scenes for a while now.

I own a share in a snooker club, the Crucible in Newbury, with two business partners who did turn out to be above and beyond what I had hoped for in people. Andy and Lyndon are more than partners in a snooker club in West Berkshire: they are true friends I would trust my life with. It's also pretty cool that I no longer have to scratch around for two shillings for the meter.

Occasionally I'll still play myself – on a Monday night with the same bunch of lads I've played with for 15 years. Well over 40, now I qualify for senior tournaments, and yes, they remind me of that too. I'm not anything like the snooker player I once was and that hurts. Age catches up with everyone.

The Plan to build the World Seniors Tour is underway and I want to take it to a place where it can become fully professional; by that I don't just mean in terms of prize money, but to make it viable enough to continue long after I've finished. I'm hopeful that will turn out to be my legacy and one day in a hundred years who knows, they might just talk about how it all started?

Has creating Snooker Legends been a success? Maybe not financially, but I've been lucky to work in a sport I love, one that I grew up playing. I didn't know that by taking my first steps at 11 years old inside the Men's Institute in Mount Hawke that it would shape my professional career in such a way.

There have been tough times; the trolling and personal abuse I suffered on social media in 2014 was shocking. Police were involved, as were Channel 5 and Frankie Bridge, who wanted to feature the story on TV. They gave me enough information for me to know who was involved, not enough to convict, so I won't name these people publicly. Their motive for such a vile campaign of hate remains unknown. Knowing certainly helps. People said ignore it, but unless you've experienced it you have no idea what it's like to live with it every day. The truth is they are cowards, keyboard warriors desperate for attention, and of course most of the time it's not personal even though it seems so. Anyone who is going through anything similar has my sympathy. Anyone who followed the story and wants to get answers themselves can start here with some Ip addresses:

91.213.8.84, 37.221.161.235, 92.122.215.76, 178.18.17.204

Or here with these phone numbers 07852764137, 07588856233, 07513140014

I am privileged, and I know what it means to have access to the stars of the game, and call them my friends. But make no mistake, I've worked bloody hard and sacrificed plenty to get here.

It wasn't always easy carrying Ronnie's cue, you know. The truth is I wish someone had been carrying mine; I wish it was me who'd been good enough to travel the world playing the game I love.

What I do isn't potting balls, but it's not a bad alternative...